REDNECK

Gravy

REDNECK
Gravy

PATRICK S. KEEFE

TWO HARBORS PRESS

Minneapolis

Two Harbors Press

212 3rd Avenue North, Suite 290

Minneapolis, MN 55401

612.455.2293

www.TwoHarborsPress.com

ISBN - 978-1-936198-80-1

ISBN - 1-936198-80-0

LCCN - 2010929677

Cover Design & Typeset by Kristeen Wegner

Printed in the United States of America

For Christopher and Liam

"Forti et Fordeli"

Table of Recipes

Preface

Back when newsrooms at local papers smelled like cigarette smoke and ink—as recently as the late '80s—denizens would occasionally speak of the standard model rumpled reporter/editor who had an unfinished typed manuscript in the bottom desk drawer alongside the half-drunk bottle of hooch. In the drama of the model, the bottle got regular, sneaking attention and replenishment, while the manuscript languished day after year after decade. The beauty of the idea was more than a few newsrooms actually had such an individual. That, together with the stereotype portrayed in almost every newspaper movie, validated its legendary authenticity. The manuscript represented the journalist's ultimate achievement: to write a book. The fact the bottle got used and renewed while the manuscript went unfinished if not forgotten, almost an embarrassment, was symptomatic of the reporter/editor. Good intentions writ large, but the press of everyday business and the need to get another paper out, plus human vice and fallibility, prevented the full flowering of the would-be author.

When I was a newspaper reporter and editor, I fully subscribed to the idea. In fact, my version was a little more piquant because I actually got assigned by the paper to write a book: an informal history of the paper in connection with its two hundredth anniversary. I was to start at the beginning in 1789 in Norwich, Connecticut, and bring the reader up to the present. It was a wonderful project. But in the scheme of things, the "book" turned into a thirty-six-page broadsheet newspaper special section, which was met relatively well. The ideal was not quite achieved, although all the vicissitudes of researching, writing, and despairing over the product were.

The ubiquity of the computer, the changing nature of journalism, news gathering, and dissemination, and the decline of the newspaper all conspired to make the model musty, dusty, and mythological, if in fact now merely a ghostly memory in today's unoccupied, shuttered, and cobwebbed newsrooms. But the model remained in my mind's eye, even as I left the newspaper business for the college news bureau.

Long a relief valve for reporters and editors seeking better wages and regular hours, the college news bureau was itself a model rapidly evolving in the world of higher education. While still writing and sending out news releases, feeding experts to local media, and informing internal and external audiences through printed products about happenings on campus, the college news bureau was transforming into a corporate communications office, adding initiatives like producing the *de rigeur* glossy quarterly magazine, taking on institutional marketing, and being responsible for and able to defend the results, adapting to and incorporating computer-based capabilities such as web pages and e-mail, and formalizing emergency public response and crisis communications. Phrases such as "stakeholders," "branding," and "reputation conservation and management" were heard frequently in the office, and the challenges were new, many, and a delight to confront and manage.

The opportunity for me to make a midlife career change was a beneficence from on high. I was already blessed with a job that was enjoyable, interesting, and adequately remunerative. I did, however, have a tedious commute, a minimum of an hour a day each way at prime time. After twenty years, the cumulative effect was irresolution, shaken nerves, and burgeoning resentment.

So when the opportunity to leave Connecticut and move to Louisiana presented itself in 2005, I was more than interested. Louisiana! Fabled land of bayous and Spanish moss, internationally acclaimed eating, "Sportsmen's Paradise," Cajun culture and music, the hedonism of Mardi Gras, the royal blue and old gold-clad Fightin' Tigers of Louisiana State University, vast riches in oil and agriculture and industry, plus darkly-intriguing New Orleans. It was also the Louisiana of endemic corruption and crazed politicians like Huey Long, institutionalized poverty, oppressive summers that begin in April and last until November, a prominent place at the bottom of lists such as "best educated," "healthiest," and "lowest crime rates," plus the incomprehensible incompetence of the elected leadership of New Orleans.

Yet good taken with bad, it was an opportunity I wanted to latch onto. When the chance became the deed in 2006, I was delighted to move. I also knew what I was going to do: Head offshore and cook on oil rigs and write a book about the experience.

What you have in your hand is the culmination of

that idea.

The title comes from an experience on my first hitch offshore as a galley hand. It was the first week early in the morning, just as dayside was coming on shift. Ken, the steward, was there and Carlos, the night cook/baker, and me. One of the bosses, an older gent named R.D. Collins, came into the galley, looked over the breakfast line, and said, "Hey y'all, can any of you make some redneck gravy?"

The cooks didn't respond but, never having heard the term before, I laughed and said, "Well probably. What is it?"

R.D. called me a confounded Yankee for not knowing what redneck gravy was, but went on to explain it was basically tomato gravy. It's a breakfast dish that you put on biscuits. He pointedly mentioned that it contained four ingredients (roux, canned tomatoes, salt, and pepper), and that under no circumstances did it contain hot sauces or salsa, ketchup, jalapenos, or "any other crap," as he put it.

I think he was making a pitch for some custom-made R.D.-style tomato gravy.

Carlos made some the next morning, but his Mexican heritage won out in the end. Or, after he tasted R.D.'s version, he didn't like it, so he doctored it up with salsa and other "crap." I tried the dish and it was OK, but I still preferred sausage gravy on biscuits.

A couple of months later I was working as a night cook on Hercules 21 when one of the bosses came in for breakfast. He too was an older gent, non-talkative, a little more Oklahoma than Louisiana or Mississippi, and cowboy thin. He asked if I could make tomato gravy. "Redneck gravy!" I exclaimed and added, "Sure!" I told him about a guy named Collins on Herc. 11. "That would be R.D. Collins," he said, demonstrating the advantage of having been a Hercules employee for thirty years. I offered to whip up a batch right then and he said, "No, tomorrow would be fine."

So I made a batch the next morning—just like R.D. described—with roux, canned tomatoes, salt, and pepper. The next day, the Okie came in, nodded a greeting, took a biscuit, cracked it open, and ladled on some gravy. He then went over to an unoccupied table and sat with his back to the galley and ate breakfast.

Finished, he bussed his tray and swung back around again to the line. "I liked that. Thank you," he said. "You're a good cook."

I nodded to acknowledge the compliment. "That's kind of you to say. I appreciate it," I replied.

I didn't make it every morning, but I did make it probably every other other morning. I liked seeing the men eat hearty, and liked being the guy who served them up good grub and redneck gravy.

CHAPTER 1

Offshore

I t's 7:20 p.m. Sunday, "Fried Chicken Day" in the Gulf of Mexico. In three hours and ten minutes, I will be serving the midnight meal to 140 hungry men. I'm all alone. Yesterday the baker, who sometimes helps out, quit and was taken off our oil rig by helicopter to shore. I have ten holes on the serving line to fill: soup; meat (fried chicken); alternative meat (meat loaf); heart-healthy main entrée (baked tilapia fillets); mashed potatoes; brown gravy; red beans; rice; four vegetables: squash, corn, mustard greens, and peas; and a trio of breakfast offerings to fill one hole with one-third pans each of grits, oatmeal, and bacon.

It's the forty-fourth time I've been the principal night cook—I'm not exactly inexperienced, but I'm not too seasoned a professional—and I'm on the sixteenth day of a twenty-one-day trip, two more than I usually do. I look around and don't see any of the usual meal items prepared by the day cook that I can use. No rice. No beans. No gravy. I'm a little surprised. "Dayside" is better staffed, and they have been very considerate about setting things aside for "nightside." There are *always* beans and rice, usually gravy,

1

and frequently vegetables. Not this time, though.

"I am so screwed," I tell myself. "You better get going. . . ."

I move fast. I have to—there's that much to do. No Louisiana dawdling pace for me. It's full speed ahead just to keep up. Full speed in my case means pretty quickly. I'm not running, but I am striding smartly. If I was a horse, I'd be at a canter.

Posters announce the midnight meal runs from 11:00 p.m. to 1:00 a.m., but usually the window opens at 10:30 and the men file into the galley from 10:15.

Plus, opening a half hour early lets them burn one or extends their change and gear-up time before shift. Being late inconveniences them. Being late can also bring a reproach from the steward or camp boss, and no one wants that. Chronic lateness doesn't happen because the chronically late cook is the fired cook. I'm trained a little differently. As a former reporter and editor, I know a deadline means your task has to be finished—so if the line opens at 10:30, the line will damn well open at 10:30.

Night shift starts at 5:00 p.m., a half hour after the supper window opens. Dayside has the meal prepared and extra food to replace what the men have eaten. But there's always something to do: deep fry French fries or pork chops; extra pans to schlep and empty ones to replace; food items to stir and keep fresh; and the line to maintain. Once dayside leaves, I'm running the place, and although the camp boss is around and always helps, his duties frequently take him elsewhere. So during mealtime, there's not much time to think about or prep for the next meal.

This galley is fairly well equipped. Although the

number of men is nearly three times as many as I usually cook for, technology is available. Best of all, it works, which isn't true for all galleys. The oven is a commercial-grade convection oven capable of holding six sheet pans. The dials haven't worn down, so you can see the temperature settings and the temperature is true. If you need 450 Fahrenheit, you can get it. Plus, with a two-speed blower, you can maximize the convection effect, which is important when you're in or about to be in trouble, also called "my life story." There's a commercial-grade steamer, which can cook, heat, or reheat vegetables, starches, or gravies and accommodate enough pans to fill four holes. And, the deep-fat fryer is a double unit, fairly new.

Once the supper meal line has been cleared, I pause in the prep spot to look at my menu and figure out how things are going to go. One rule I've learned in the galley is: water, water, water. Boiling water. By the gallon. I need water for the mashed potatoes. I need it for rice. I need it for the grits and oatmeal. I'm going to need it for the beans. I don't like hefting huge pots of water—at a little more than eight pounds a gallon, a five-gallon pot weighs in excess of forty pounds. I'm moving fast, but the option of putting the pot on the stove, then filling it with two or three kettles of a gallon or two each is insane. No time! So I fill a five-gallon pot in the sink and heft it over to the stove. There's no good way to do this. Grab the handles and pick it up using your legs, trying to preserve your back. You're using your arms and shoulders, your stomach, and vulnerable lower back muscles, and you're walking like the weirdos you see on the sidewalks in New Orleans. It's sheer strength, which is why chefs are usually very strong, though many suffer from ruined backs. I put on a couple of mid-sized pots with three gallons or so each, saving the fourth burner for beans.

Just to force myself to move as fast as possible, I put the pan on empty. The burner is on full blast—about eight hundred degrees—so I've got to work maniacally to get the seasoning in before something bad happens—like the pan overheating and wrecking everything. A couple of nights ago, I couldn't find any oil. "Cripes, how do you run a kitchen with no oil?" I fume and end up taking a quarter cup out of the deep fryer. The oil is OK because it was changed after "Seafood Day." Tonight I know where the oil lives (under the prep counter) and I douse the pot with some. Grab a couple of green peppers and a couple of onions, dice the peppers and get them into the oil, go back, cut the onions like a Food Network chef (cutting half through the stem, peeling quickly, and slicing horizontally three times using the flat of my hand to anchor it to the cutting board, then slicing it five or six times at a ninety-degree angle to the root, and finally making thin slices parallel to the root), which produces a beautiful dice in about as much time as it takes to tell about it.

The onions go in, I grab a smoked pork shank out of the freezer and drop it in, open two one-pound bags of red beans, pick them over quickly in a colander under running water, and dump them in. Stir, dump in a load of black pepper, Tony Chachere's spice seasoning, and enough water to cover everything, and clap on a lid. It's 7:30 and they'll be done at 10:00.

I'm fair-to-good on my chicken. Figuring six pieces per roaster, I've got eight whole birds thawed, but I need more. I rummage around in the freezer and come up with a ten-pound bag of legs and thighs. Good, but it's frozen. I bring it to the sink, stuff a rag into the drain, and fill it with cold water to advance the thaw.

I put on my hand mail to cut the whole birds. I use my cleaver, which was professionally sharpened in Baton Rouge before I left home, and it's pretty good going. I cut the birds in half, parallel to the breast bone and down just adjacent to the back bone. I cut out the backbone—good for stock—then take off the wings and legs. I nip off the wing tip—ditto, stock—and do a pretty serious hack job on the thigh. I get the joint on the drumstick OK, but the thigh is tricky. I think to myself, "You need some practice getting this right."

The pieces go into a tub for washing when I'm done. I dump the tub of bird in the sink under running water to clean it and make sure there are no bone fragments. I take the cleaned pieces and put them back into the tub after shaking them. I'm just using spice and a few eggs, together with the residual rinse water, on the birds as the marinade. There are legions of stories in galleys about the best marinade and certain ingredients that will wreck the oil. However, the consensus appears to be that water is good and buttermilk is best, but it can wreck the oil. Water and spice it is for me tonight.

It's 7:50. Ay, caramba! The oil! Dayside used the oil in the fryer to cook up a bunch of chicken for the noon meal. I've got to strain it before I use it. And although I've done that countless times and have the bugs worked out, it's still going to take twenty minutes. I turn the heating elements off and take the baskets out. The first time I cleaned a fryer on another rig, I pulled the heating element up and locked it into place. The power was still on, and in seconds the element was smoking and turning adhered bits of coating and fryer debris into a tiny flame. The galley hand, white faced, croaked, "Flames!" I had a millisecond's vision of having to hit the emergency fire extinguisher and dumping a whole system's worth of foam on the fryer, the range, the grill, and stove. Imagine cleaning up *that* mess! But my next thought was: "Lose the oxygen!" I unlocked the element and plunged it back into the oil, extinguishing the flame. Learning from my mistake, this time, like every next time, I make sure the power is off before lifting the element out of the oil.

Once the oil's drained, I scrub out the inside of the fryer. I'm working fast, but I'm also burning precious minutes. When one fryer is clean, I pour the strained oil back in and repeat the procedure on the second. It's a pain, but I'll be in good shape for the chicken and French fries. I'm done at 8:20, two hours and ten minutes until the line opens.

I stir my red beans, check on my heating water, and set up for the vegetables. I cut open industrial-sized packages of squash, corn, mustard greens, and peas, and dump them into pans. I add a heaping tablespoon of chicken broth concentrate, a stick of margarine, and water to each just to the top of the veggies. I cover the pans with plastic wrap and load them into the steamer. It takes forty minutes to steam them from solid, and it's now 8:30, so I turn it on.

Time to assess where we be. Looking over the menu, not very damn good.

Soup: OK. Dayside made a nice beef and vegetable that can run again.

Fish: Undone. Do it now.

I search the fridge, but there is none thawing. Zipping into the freezer, I locate the case and take it over to the sink. I grab a five-gallon pot and start filling it with cold water to help the thaw while counting out two dozen—no, thirty—frozen tilapia filets. We'll have baked tilapia with Italian seasoning. It's tasty; it's easy; and the convection oven at four hundred with full blowers on can do it in ten minutes.

It's 8:37. Back to assessing.

Next: Chicken. OK.

It's marinating. I figure forty pieces to open the line, four batches of ten pieces each. That could be too much for the fryers. The oil needs to circulate. But I can take the baskets out and let them float free-style in the fryer. I figure possibly ten per fryer per batch. If the second batch comes out just before the line opens, then it goes on at 10:05. So the first should go in at 9:40. Breading has to be made and . . . my eye sees the next item: meatloaf. Aaaiieeah! I gotta get going! "Wait, no need to panic . . . yet. If the burger is thawed, you're OK," I counsel myself. It is, three five-pound rolls. Thanks be to St. Lawrence, the patron saint of cooks, and to St. Jude, my patron and the patron saint of hopeless and lost causes. Assessment be danged; it's time to make the meatloaf. Brain jumps ahead. "Figure seven or eight pounds. It's got to fill the hole on the line and look substantial in a pan. Yep, two of 'em. And if the guys don't eat it, well-cooked burger has lots of uses."

Grabbing an industrial-sized stainless steel bowl, I cut open the burger and drop it in. It looks like a lot. Visualizing what I'm going to have, I downsize my plan because with the onion, eggs, and breadcrumbs, it looks like one package should be plenty. A nice-rounded thick loaf with a tomato dressing and some gravy will present well in the pan and should feed at least twenty. And this is Fried Chicken Night, after all.

At home, I usually sauté the onions before adding them, but this is going to cook for an hour or more, so I omit the step and save time. The meatloaf won't change my plans for the convection oven, either, because I won't cook the fish until after 10:00. If I get it in now, 8:43, it can cook for an hour easily before it's time to fret about the fish. I grab a couple of big white onions, TV chef-dice them, and toss them in the bowl. I crack in four eggs and a cup of breadcrumbs and start to mix it with my fingers. The meatloaf looks soupy and anemic, so I tear off my latex gloves, dash off to the veggie locker, grab a green pepper, wash it and dice it with a cleaver in my best imitation of a professional Chinese chef. That goes in with a generous pour of breadcrumbs, plus some garlic, Worcestershire sauce, Tony Chachere's Cajun seasoning, and black pepper, all of which produces a better texture. I grab a sheet pan and a long piece of tin foil. The foil will make washing the pan easier for the galley hand and help keep the meatloaf together. I've seen a meatloaf fall apart and that's not decent, but by crumpling some foil fore and aft of the loaf, and on the sides if it's really desperate, you improve your chances of it coming out in a loaf instead of a steaming mound. I spray the foil with cooking spray and dump the bowl onto the foil. I pat it into shape, dam it up with foil, and slide it on a middle rack into the oven at four hundred. I look at the clock. It's 8:55. That's not so good, but I'm better off than I was ten minutes ago.

I check the beans and give them a stir. Good. My water is beginning to boil. Time to assess by holes on the line:

1. Soup: Good.

2. Heart-healthy: Fish. OK. Thawing. Got time there.

3. Main dish: Chicken. OK. Need to make the breading.

4. Rice and beans: OK. Beans are on. Need to make rice. But I've got water on, and I'll make a load so dayside has some too.

5. and 6. Veggies: squash, corn, mustard greens, and peas. OK. I've got orange and yellow and two greens. So in one hole I'll have mustard greens and corn, and in the other I'll have squash and peas. OK.

7. Mashed potatoes and gravy: Need to make both. Water's on, and I can do it, but I've got to get going. Gravy, ditto.

8. Alternative meat: OK. Meatloaf is in the oven and is more or less on time.

9. French fries: They're frozen. I can do two baskets in five minutes. If I put them out just before opening up, it should work out OK.

10. Breakfast stuff: This is the midnight meal, and some guys are just going on shift, so we offer breakfast, too. One-third pans of oatmeal, grits, and sausage. I'm OK there. I've got water for the oats and grits, and I can throw a dozen sausage links into the oven when the fish goes in.

HAMBURGERS!

Like most rigs, this one has an "open grill," which means you can sort of get what you want from the grill. "Sort of" because for breakfast it means eggs to order, an omelet, or a grilled cheese sandwich. On midnight, it means hamburgers and cheeseburgers. Burgers are available for noon and supper, too, but "sort of" comes into play because if you asked for a fried egg or a grilled cheese sandwich at noon or supper, you might get it. But better not ask, or you might get a sandwich on your plate and a chef's cleaver in your forehead. "There's enough to eat on the line, Jasper!"

On smaller rigs, burgers count as a midnight meal main offering. Not here. You fill the ten holes *and* have burgers ready. I prefer making burgers to order, but this rig is too big for that—you could have six guys out of ten ask for one, you never know. Cooking that many would be too much of a cluster jumble out front, so we cook them just before the line opens and keep them warm on the grill.

But I've got to make and cook burgers. I've also got to make the chicken, spuds and gravy, fish, oats and grits, and sausage, and the clock is ticking.

The burger left over from the meatloaf will do perfectly at about three pounds. I dump what's left of it into a bowl and add seasoning—garlic powder, Worcestershire, Tony Chachere's, and black pepper—and mix it with my hands. I place a folded sheet of parchment on a half pan and begin to form patties. The burgers here are large—when I'm making to-order burgers, I use a half-cup to standardize the burger. That amount makes a nice burger of sufficient heft that still cooks in a few minutes. This rig makes huge burgers—a third of a pound or so. That takes a long time to grill. I make fifteen and use up what's left. It's 9:05. A little too early to start them. But soon.

Next up: rice.

Making rice on a rig puts to bed forever all the fevers some home cooks break into at the prospect of serving some. We make industrial amounts, but the technique holds for the home cook or enthusiast too. Take a big pot of water, three gallons or so, and bring it to a boil. Add a palmful of salt. Add rice to the boiling water (I use three scoops tonight, maybe fifteen cups) and set the timer for seventeen minutes. Stir the rice when it goes into the water to keep the grains separated and stir it occasionally. Start tasting it after ten minutes to check the consistency and pay attention to the timer. Seventeen minutes is right, but tasting means you won't overcook it. The rice should be cooked but firm with just a slight resistance to the bite. When it's right, dump the rice into a colander in the sink and rinse it thoroughly under cold water. That stops the cooking and washes off the starch that can make clumpy rice later. Rig workers don't like clumpy rice.

To reheat, run it under hot water, microwave, or, as here, put it in a pan and put it on the steam table.

While the rice is cooking, I can get going on the fish. The buzzer on the steamer goes off announcing that the veggies are done. They're fine, and I'll just let them sit for now. I stir the rice—it's coming along—and stride off to the oven to check on the meatloaf. Ditto.

I fish out the fillets from the pot where they're thawing and they feel OK. I take a sheet pan, line it with parchment, and grab the kitchen shears. Scissors or shears are a must in the galley, to my mind. The packaging on most products is durable, industrially resistant to mere human strength, yet I'm not too keen on slicing packages with a knife. Too much can go wrong, and it's an easy way to slice yourself. With shears you minimize that risk. The fillets are vacuum packed, so I cut them where the vacuum ends and extract the fish. I lay them out on the sheet pan, sprinkle them lightly with lemon pepper and Italian bread crumbs, and place them to the side. It takes eight minutes.

It's 9:15. I stir the rice and taste it. It's coming, but it's not ready yet.

Breading is next. The basic recipe is a two-to-one flour to cornmeal ratio with some seasonings to accent flavor: salt and pepper, Tony Chachere's. I've got about fifty pieces of chicken, so I need a couple of batches. Figure four cups of flour and two of cornmeal. I grab a medium stainless bowl and roughly measure in the flour. Same with the cornmeal. Spices go on top, then I mix it with my hands. It's not quite time for the chicken, and I don't want to bread it too far in advance of cooking because the breading could become saturated, so I get my work station set up. I tote the tub of marinating chicken over to where I'll be, pour half the breading into a whole pan, find a screening rack, insert, and lay it crosswise atop the pan. That's where I'll set the chicken after breading, so the excess can fall off and be reused. The breading pan goes to the right of the tub of chicken. I snatch a sheet pan and lay a piece of parchment on it and place it to the right of the breading. That will be where I lay the chicken, and it will serve as the tray to convey it over to the fryer.

It's 9:20. It's getting time for the rice to finish. I still need to make potatoes, gravy, oats, and grits. I check the beans. They're coming along, a little hard still, but they taste good. I move them to the side where they can still cook, but not as vigorously. The rice is almost done. A couple of minutes should do. Gravy next. Since it's fried chicken, there won't be any drippings, but that's OK. I'm a decent saucier, and there are plenty of options. The best option this time is chicken flavor concentrate. It's a million percent sodium, so you have to be temperate, but it works, and with some doctoring, it can be OK. I take a half cup of flour and half a stick of margarine and put it in a four-quart pan. Start with a roux and go from there. While the margarine is melting, I check the rice: ahh, maybe a minute more. I'm inclined to get some other stuff going, grains and spuds, but in a second I'll be busy enough, so stick with the plan.

The rice is done. And the roux is cooking. I need to work fast so the roux doesn't burn. I add a little hot water to cool things down, then grab the rice pot and heft it to the sink. I take a colander and pour the rice into it, with water from the faucet rinsing the rice and cooling it down. I mix the rice with my fingers and taste a few grains. Good. No clumps.

It's 9:27. I stop by the fryer to make sure it's on. It's not, so I switch it on and adjust the temperature to 325 degrees. No problem there. I've got thirteen minutes or so till I start frying, sufficient time to bring the oil up to temperature. Quickly back to the roux. Usually I make white gravy with chicken, but the former night cook/baker said the men prefer brown gravy. I stir the roux and water—it's hot—grab a half-gallon measuring pitcher, and race out front to the milk dispenser. Fill the pitcher. Back to the stove. Before adding the milk, I spoon in some chicken concentrate and stir it around. I add milk and whisk. It's yellow-green from the concentrate, an unusual color that if served up could queer someone's reputation offshore! I add a little Kitchen Bouquet to adjust the color. It looks like brown gravy now. I keep whisking and it's beginning to thicken. Needs pepper, but not now.

Time to get the chicken ready. I use the "wet hand,

dry hand method" of avoiding the dreaded "club hand" when layers of breading and wash build up on the cook's hand until it's the size of the Hulk's paws. Not only is it heavy and impossible to work with, it wastes foodstuffs, can frighten small dogs, traumatize toddlers, and takes way longer than it should to wash off. Avoid club hand at all costs.

With my right hand, I take a piece of chicken out of the tub and place it in the flour, turning it to coat it evenly. With my left, I "splash" breading over the bare spots. I use my right to knock it against the side of the pan, jarring any excess loose before placing it on the rack. When the rack is full with about a dozen pieces, I move them to the sheet pan. Another eight or ten pieces and my first batch is done. I've got a good mix of wings and thighs and breasts and drumsticks.

The green light is on, meaning both fryers are at temperature. The baskets come out and go on the rack underneath, and ten pieces of chicken go into each fryer. I drop one piece of chicken into each fryer quickly so it's all done at once. The timer is set for twenty minutes. It's 9:43.

Forty-five minutes before the line opens. Enough time to start filling holes. It'll help with assessment, too. I know I still need fish, potatoes, grains, and sausage, plus more chicken. I roll down the sectioned steel curtain that screens the galley from the dining area. The curtain serves a couple of purposes: It lets me fill the line in peace and it keeps pilferers out. Breakfast is the best time for pilfering sausages and strips of bacon, but the supper line is vulnerable, too, especially on fried chicken night.

I turn the steam table on and make sure all the holes have water in them. They don't. Most are low and a couple are empty. The steam table works by heating water to make steam to heat the food in pans set above the water. Like a double boiler. The table has standardized dimensions so various combinations of pans can be assembled, and the pans themselves come in various depths, so the amount they hold can be prodigious. In fact, the bases of the steam table are eight- or ten-inch deep pans that permanently reside there. In the two and a half hours the line is open each meal, a lot of water gets turned into steam. It's important to replenish the water because without it, you won't have steam.

It's 9:46. Steam table filled. I start to fill holes. I take the four veggie pans out of the steamer and load up holes five and six. Temp is on full blast; I turn it down to half. OK. They're done.

Hole one is filled with the soup. I adjust the temperature and it's done.

I take a half pan, lubricate it with spray, and fill it with rice. That's half of hole four. I fill the other half by filling a pan with beans and plunking it down. That's one, four, five, and six filled.

I take a skimmer and poke at the chicken. It's coming along. I look at the meatloaf. It needs time, too.

It's 9:50. I take empty pans and fill the remaining holes so I can visualize what's coming. Two is fish; three is chicken. Both get whole pans. Seven is mashed potatoes and gravy, so it gets half pans. Eight is meatloaf and nine is French fries, so they get whole pans. Ten is breakfast. It gets one-third pans.

The meatloaf is at 375, and I can use that temperature to cook the fish as well. Both blowers are on, and it's a hot 375. I'll have to be careful with the fish, but I'm not too

15

worried about overcooking. Rarely do you get a complaint about overcooking. You're much more likely to hear about something undercooked, so put the fire right to it! That's what I do with the burgers. Since they're gigantic, they'll need a lot of cooking. But I don't want to incinerate them, merely cook them until, well, they're "rig done." Figure seventeen minutes at 350.

The grill is on, all three elements set to temperature, and I lay out the burgers.

Take a poke at the chicken with the strainer to make sure pieces are separated. Some are floating, meaning it's coming along and it's time to get the fish in.

I put the fish in the oven, check the time, and consider the meatloaf. I'm going to leave it in. I poke it with a finger and it seems firm, but I'm more comfortable with it being slightly overcooked than even slightly undercooked.

The timer goes off. The first batch of chicken is done. It's 10:03 and I'm OK—not great—but OK. I fish out the chicken and turn around to load up hole number three. There's a decent pile of chicken and it looks nice: a lovely golden brown color. I grab a wing and bite into it. Bravo! Not only does it taste good, and have a quality fried chicken crackle, but it's cooked! The green light is on, meaning the oil is at temperature, and I quickly drop the next batches into the fryers. It's 10:05. Set the timer. Time for spuds and grains.

Rig oatmeal is instant and cooks itself. I don't make too much because there's not much market for it. It's really a throw-away proposition on midnights.

I grab a medium pot and pour in four cups of water. I throw in a couple cups of oatmeal and a pinch of salt, stir it, cover it, and pull it off the range. I'm a little more fastidious about my grits because I want them to be good, but they're not so popular on nights either. They don't need constant attention, just careful attention. I take another medium pot and pour in ten cups of water. That'll use two-and-a-half-cups of grits and will make a substantial amount, but it won't be too wasteful if it doesn't sell well. I add some salt and measure in the grits. I whisk them to keep them separated and move it so it's partially over the element. Grits have to cook, but I don't want them blasted over 750 degrees.

Time for the spuds. Instant mashed can go from good to lousy in an instant. There's a point in adding liquid when the spuds transform from granules into solid clumps of off-putting material. That material is potential mashed potatoes, but the transitive phase is truly frightening. If you're of nervous temperament or physically weak, faced with the indefinable glutinous mass, you just might give it up and surrender. But then your obit will read, "Defeated by the spuds, he cast himself overboard and was last seen drown-proofing in the direction of Antigua . . ."

When the instant spuds are at their worst, they're almost ready. For the stout-hearted, the addition of more liquid seems the prescription. Something to tame the snarling clump that has wrenched your whisk from your hand and is now heavy and ominous and only inches from your face in your twenty-inch stainless steel bowl. But here the stout-hearted need courage, because the addition of a drop too much liquid will de-clump the mass and turn your spuds into soup.

This has happened to me sufficiently that I'm aware of the peril. At the risk of rotator cuff and elbow displacement, I continue to whisk with force, adding liquid by the drop to achieve the consistency I want. I season them with chicken broth concentrate and pepper and put them in their hole that, together with the half pan of gravy, fills hole seven. I drizzle some margarine over the top and a few sprinkles of parsley. They look good and taste OK.

I flip the burgers, then step back to the stove to stir the grits. They're about ready so into the hole they go. I pour the oatmeal into its container and that goes in hole ten too. There's a third pan awaiting sausage that I'll do last.

Things are shaping up, but the clock's marching relentlessly on. It's 10:15.

Fish and meatloaf next. I poke the chicken to keep it separated and stride on to the oven. I've learned to keep my face out of the way when opening the oven to avoid the blast of hot air that's uncomfortable, but more importantly, fogs up your glasses and slows you down. No time for slow!

The fish is nice, cooked but not incinerated, and the meatloaf is firm. I grab the place holder pan out of hole two and take it and the pan of fish to the workbench. I line the pan with parchment paper and place the fillets in two by two. I cut a few slices of lemon and garnish the fish with them.

Burgers are done, meaning they're cooked until dry. I take a four-inch-deep half pan, pour in a couple tablespoons of Kitchen Bouquet and add a splash of water. That'll provide some liquid flavor for the burgers to swim in and give the pretence that they're juicy. I scoop the burgers off the grill into the pan.

It's 10:25. The chicken is done. I run to the oven to get the meatloaf and bring it over to the workbench. I need a tomato garnish, and it looks sort of bare so some juice in the pan would help. I pour some liquid from the cooking pan into the serving pan and bring it over to the line. I add a little gravy and carefully twist the pan around and around to mix them. I run to the fridge and grab a bag of fries and a package of sausage. I kick the door shut and hotfoot it to the fryer to put in the fries. I tear open the sausage links box and dump them into the basket then launch it into the fryer too. It's 10:28.

I grab a small stainless bowl, dump in a cup of ketchup, some Worcestershire sauce, and some Tony Chachere's, whisk it and pour it on top of the meatloaf for garnish. I make my way up the line, placing the appropriate serving utensil into the serving pans and removing the plastic wrap from the veggies in holes five and six.

It's 10:30 and I'm ready to go. The fries and sausage will be done in seconds, and the line is filled and looking good. A great meal. Chicken and mashed with gravy, soup, heart-healthy fish, rice and beans, veggies, meatloaf, and burgers are ready. I'll open first, then fill the fries and sausage in holes nine and ten while the men make their way down the line.

I roll up the steel curtain and lock it in place with a screwdriver. There are ten guys in line.

"Morning gents," I call out. "Sunday night in the Gulf. Fried Chicken Night! Come and get it!"

Mission accomplished.

The third guy in line asks for a burger and another gent asks for a cheeseburger. "Can do," I say and start to make them.

I'm pretty proud. Feelin' good! Like Emeril says,

"It's cooking, not rocket science." But the grub is good; I opened on time; I overcame some deficiencies and, of course, I worked my ass off.

"Yes sir!" I'm thinking, "I'm the cat's nazz!"

"Hey, gimme a couple over easy," some cretin calls. Moron. Mental midget. That order deflates my ego like an earthquake flattens a soufflé. That's right, cookie, you're all prepped up for Fried Chicken Night in the Gulf, but it's also breakfast. Remember? That's why you made oats and grits and sausage. Open grill at midnight and that means eggs to order.

The eggs I don't have.

Shoulders slumping, I head for the fridge to retrieve a rack.

CHAPTER 2

Background

My name is Patrick Keefe and I'm Dover, New Hampshire, born and bred. I've always been interested in food, for good or ill, since I was a kid. As an adult, when the chance presented itself to change careers and work as a cook on an oil rig in the Gulf of Mexico, I latched onto it firmly.

The opportunity was unusual. My career to that point had revolved around news gathering, reporting and editing, and, subsequently, public information, institutional communications, and spokesman tasks. My cooking skills were of a "hobbyist" or "enthusiast" level, but I thought that counted at least as much as those of the professional level whose attitude, eroded by time and drudgery, produced a jaded, weary, or apathetic individual. Food thoughtfully prepared and well-cooked—even if the raw material was institutional quality—would be superior to some hash house slop thrown together by the uncaring, I reasoned.

No way could I or would I throw something together. Even if it was what later came to be called jambalaya, it was never inadvertent—ingredients haphazardly assembled.

The ingredients needed compatibility, or at least affinity, and the combination of the ingredients needed to evoke a foreseeable prospect of tasting decent.

Such was not always the case in the Keefe family household. As an Irish-American scion, I was a solid meat and potatoes kid. My favorite meal was roast pork, roast potatoes, gravy, and Mott's applesauce. That meal could be elevated to heavenly ambrosia with the addition of Cushman's brown 'n' serve rolls, but that rarely, if ever, occurred. I could easily sit at the kitchen table Friday nights well after supper, commanded to remain there until finished, with picked-at shrimp casserole in front of me while my parents and sister in the living room watched Don Ameche and International Showtime. Tomato was a marginal substance—OK if disguised in Franco-American spaghetti out of the can, but poisonous by itself in a salad or wretched in clumps in American goulash. Picking out the clumps rendered goulash halfway decent, with hamburger and elbow macaroni and some other flavors boiled into insensibility. MMMmmm. Bland and not too tasty. Most green things were filthy. Green peas taught my father a lesson about forcing a seven-year-old to eat his vegetables, when appetites around the Sunday dinner table were suddenly and totally extinguished by said seven-year-old gagging and bolting away from the table to disgorge that teaspoonful of peas and a bellyful of chum over the porch railing.

While my family members surely weren't gourmets of any renown, they ate well. My grandmother, Margaret Kilcoyne Wallace, was a cook for wealthy Yankees when she emigrated to New Hampshire from the Old Country of Ireland in the early twentieth century. I think she learned a lot from the regular staff. I can't imagine Yankees hiring a peasant Irish girl with limited experience to cook for them. What's she going to make? Cockles? Oatmeal? Poteen?

My grandfather, her husband, also a Mick émigré, was a Boston and Maine Railroad laborer with plain meat and potatoes taste. Hardworking and thrifty, he gardened and Margaret put up his produce for the winter. The Wallaces ate well, if not spectacularly, even during the Depression, when the neighbors were eating popcorn for breakfast and supper with no lunch.

Both my mother and her sister, my aunt Mary, were good cooks, having learned at the hand of their mother. My aunt was adventuresome. She specialized in exotic desserts à la Julia Child, making Sunday afternoon at the grandparents' in nearby Rochester, New Hampshire, sumptuous. Utilitarian in tastes, I liked cakes, cupcakes, and cookies, despite baked Alaska and flambé.

My father's people were lace-curtain Irish, so they ate notionally better. My father summered at "the farm," and he had a taste for unpasteurized milk, cream, and fresh corn and tomatoes, as well as martinis and manhattans, steak with butter, and baked potatoes oozing sour cream. As an adult, he wasn't above pottering about in the kitchen, but it was occasional and sporadic. Every now and then, he'd make spaghetti sauce that cooked over the oil range for so long it was purple and bitter, but we liked it, or at least we thought we did. He also made a respectable shrimp cocktail sauce for Thanksgiving and Christmas that introduced me tangentially to the concept of "spiciness."

I was interested in what was happening in the kitchen from a young age. I remember helping my mother make pie crust, and I got to make "tarts" out of leftover dough and strawberry jam. I was intrigued with her "headache band," a piece of clean sheet dipped in milk and tied around the pie crust to keep it from scorching. Now there's a piece of wood-stove Mick cookery, if ever there was!

I helped her make cakes and frosting and cookies, not just for the maternal interaction, or to glom onto the spoons and bowls for licking (Although that did matter!)—but it was interesting. Early on, I knew how to boil potatoes and spaghetti.

Thanksgiving was a special day, and I'd get up with her at 4:00 or 4:30 a.m. to prepare the bird and get it in the oven. I knew how to season and stuff a bird, and after it was in and my mother returned to bed, I'd go out for a walk and to sneak a Raleigh filter cigarette or two on the deserted streets of town. Thanksgiving dawn, regardless of weather, always portended a good time for a ten-year-old.

I'd help out in the kitchen at my grandparents' home, too. My grandmother was always cooking and, like all grandmothers, her fresh-made bread had to be eaten to be believed. For whatever reason, my specialty visiting them in Rochester was gingerbread cake and gingerbread men cookies. It was winter food, not a year-round offering. At nine or ten years old, I knew the scratch recipe by heart and could rip off a cake in ninety minutes or so, and frequently did.

Odd.

My culinary interest was furthered when I got a part-time job with Soldati Catering in Exeter. The Soldatis were a renowned Italian family from Somesworth, a small town adjacent to Dover. There were at least four boys and three girls, and there might've been more I never met. The males from the earliest days worked for their father as stone masons. The boy laborers, hauling stone, setting brick, and mixing cement, capitalized on quality Etruscan stock and developed muscles of monumental proportion. They took time off from work during the fall to anchor the high school football team on the line and in the backfield, leading tiny Somesworth to improbable football state championships.

After the war, one of the middle brothers, Lincoln, returned home and with another brother, Pacifico "Sol" Soldati, established an Italian restaurant in Durham, home of the University of New Hampshire. The restaurant served some of the first pizzas in New Hampshire to the UNH students. The brothers gave that up after a number of years, but Linc continued in the food business as a caterer, food service manager, and chef. By the late 1960s, he was a well-established caterer, his green step-van with white lettering, "Soldati Catering, Exeter, N.H." was a fixture at important St. Thomas Aquinas High School football games, purveying hot dogs, drinks and chips, hot cocoa, coffee, and doughnuts for chilled spectators.

The student organization Key Club supplied volunteer help. As a Key Club member, I was detailed to work at the St. Thomas/Portsmouth High School game. It was a big venue, and the half-time rush was quite intense. But Boss (Linc) Soldati and Sol kept things going even while the high school boys horsed around and flirted with the female schoolmate customers.

Several Key Club cutups turned the comic volume so high even the older men joined in. The experience was such fun that I volunteered to do it again. I could make change from my years as a bread delivery boy; I was quick with service; and I joined in the patter about "Gettin' 'em in and gettin' 'em out," having a good time while still making a buck.

The Key Club liaison to Soldati was Gary "Zippy" Zimmerman of Exeter, who was two years ahead of me and a classmate of my sister's. I caught Zimmerman's eye and he made some medicine with the Boss. Zippy asked if I was interested in going to Exeter to work for the company. Being young and innocent and naïve, and not knowing it was the food service gig I was getting into, I said, "Sure." My father knew Linc Soldati from long ago, called Exeter to do legal and parent best practices, and come the weekend, I became a caterer.

I didn't quite know what to expect. What I found was a residence. The driveway curved around the back of the house so the catering truck could be parked adjacent to the rear door to load and unload food and supplies. The cellar of the house served as kitchen, warehouse, and staging area, and the kitchen held a commercial eight-burner, two-oven gas stove and a built-in five-door, commercial-grade refrigerator. There were stainless steel work tables, pots, and pans from household size to ten- or twelve-gallon monsters, a glittering, deadly-looking stainless steel meat slicer, shelves of spices and ingredients, a rack of every sized knife known to man, and a Hobart industrial-size mixer. Also available were a washer and dryer, an industrial-sized two-bowl sink, a bathroom with shower, two freezers, and racks and racks of plates, cups, saucers, stemware, glasses, serving bowls and platters, chaffing dishes, centerpieces, and all the miscellany necessary to get a meal for three hundred to the banquet hall and into party-goers' stomachs.

It was a well run and flexible business. We could do two considerable events on a Saturday or even four events simultaneously, depending on their size and scope—an à la carte banquet for many; a couple of medium to small family style banquets; and a concession stand at an auction. If the events catered resulted in empty racks of dishes and silverware, we could meet most any challenge by renting supplemental equipment, borrowing Sol's wagon and pick-up, and possibly even renting a van for the day.

Lots of prep work and most of the logistics fell to Zimmerman. I helped. The Boss did most of the cooking, although he was always instructing. Once he was comfortable with a youngster's finished product, he'd delegate. He always made the marinara, the red sauce that was the basis of most of the Italian dishes we served—spaghetti, lasagne, ravioli—and its doneness was assessed by the group sampling a "dynamite," a hunk of fresh Italian bread torn off a loaf and dipped into the simmering brew. "Dynamite, Boss!" we'd all report, confirming the sauce was done and establishing a tradition.

In a relatively short period of time, we developed my specialty, concessionaire, derived from working the football games. The Boss had a weekly gig at the auction house in Hudson, New Hampshire. He'd make a five-gallon jug of coffee, take some donuts or cookies, a case of soda, some chips, candy bars, and gum, and steam a couple dozen hot dogs. That would make him $20 or so in 1969 dollars. It wasn't all work. He'd also buy stuff at the auction, the value of which he'd proclaim loudly saying, "A good deal. This is a good deal, Pat!" Generally, appreciation of these treasures eluded me.

Being at the auction gave him an "in" to New Hampshire's auction community so to speak, a vigorous and active world of commerce and trade that arose out of Yankee thrift, the hatred of seeing something useful go to waste, and just-plain-penny-pinching. Auctions were favored ways to settle estates, or dispose of trash and treasure alike. An all-day affair at some eighteenth century farmhouse in Hampton would ensure bargain hunters, antique seekers, the curious, and neighbors seeking revenge for a lifetime's abrasion by the old crank, achieving redemption and victory by purchasing a formerly beloved dresser for $50 less than it was worth.

The auction-goers needed to eat, and the Boss figured we'd feed them. An association with Smith and Mankiewicz auctioneers from up Henniker way opened the state for us, and the auction concession initiative took on a life of its own. S&M was a well known, reputable firm with auctions about every weekend from May through September. Their expertise brought them to cities and towns across the state, with Soldati's truck, or the "Warhorse," a 1965 blue Ford Country Squire station wagon with a 390-cubic-inch-engine as accompaniment.

As the auction work became more consistent, the menu improved. A gas grill on wheels added hamburgers and cheeseburgers to the steamed hot dog menu. A used refrigerator, secured to the interior rear of the truck, instantly produced new vistas of vending: ice creams and frozen confections; sandwiches (egg salad, tuna salad, chicken salad) that contained mayo and needed to be refrigerated; and lettuce, tomato, and onions for torqued-up burgers with a fifteen-cent price increase. The refrigerator also ensured safer transportation of perishables.

Along with the innovation came a new series of skills. Counterman and concessionaire, in addition to planning, preparing, packing, and steaming hot dogs, now had to be a short-order cook. Prep evolved from ensuring there was a variety of candy bars to boiling and picking chickens, learning to perfect hard-cooked eggs, and making sure the tuna wasn't too "wet" with mayo, plus ensuring there was a cooked ham for ham and cheese and a roast beef for sandwiches on Kaiser rolls.

The Boss helped with all of this. He'd often cook the beef or ham or boil a chicken during the week so I had raw materials when I went to work Fridays after school. But the mixing and the making was my job.

One distinct advantage of working at Soldati's Catering was you ate well. The Boss was a generous man and a great cook. His pasta was perfectly cooked at a time long before al dente was a demand on the lips of children. His lasagne was thick, moist, and a perfect quartet of meat, cheese, pasta, and sauce. His "Italian" roast beef was a show stopper at banquets or weddings, the beef cooked medium-medium rare and flavored with a mix of spices I can only conjecture. Garlic was one for sure, the rest are lost to food history. But to get a piece of crust crunchy with sear and spices was a notable experience for food enthusiast or a meat and potatoes kid.

One other staff favorite was his "lumberjack's breakfast." It didn't happen just anywhere. It usually came about after an unusual or weird occasion: a night camping in the Warhorse in the mountains of New Hampshire to get a head start on an event in far Berlin; the morning of the second day at a two day auction; or maybe grabbing an hour off to eat at dawn after an all-dark start for a hundred-mile trip to Claremont. Lumberjack's breakfast was meat, potatoes, eggs, and toast. Depending on his mood and insulin needs, the boss might add something else, from Bermuda onions to apples in the mix, but it usually worked.

Conversations were what you might expect between a forty-eight-year-old and a seventeen-year-old.

"Sknnnrggggkkkyzzzzz!" would say the Boss, inhaling mightily and drinking in that sweet New Hampshire dawn. "I've got a lumberjack breakfast coming here, uh, uh, uh, Pat!"

"Hunh?" was the adenoidal response.

"That's right, just like they serve in the lumber camps in uh, uh, uh Maine! Or the Allagash! That's right, up in the Allagash! Steak and eggs and potato and garlic!" The latter ingredient was probably a breakfast surprise to the lumberjacks in Maine who might've thought the Allagash was a part of their state.

"Look at this," he'd say, thick arm thrown out encompassing the kingdom, "God's work."

Indeed. But to a yout' most mountain scenes are just hills and trees and low-lying clouds, not vast expressions of divine beneficence, and, more importantly, is there any ketchup for the spuds?

Lumberjack's breakfast once experienced was not to be forgotten, because the food, the setting, and the circumstances were so unusual. But youth, secure in the wisdom of ignorance, can transform the notable into the mundane. Or as a young caterer once replied, "Jeez, Boss. I feel more like the lumber!"

Background

I quit catering in 1971 to return to college in Minnesota. Unsurprisingly, higher education involves more than intramural sports, pinochle, and slugging 3.2 beer and Ripple Pagan Pink wine. Reality caught up with me in late September when, without classes or tuition money, I left school and returned to New Hampshire to join the army.

Cooking became important in a new way in 1973. Crowded barracks and VolAr, the Volunteer Army initiative following the cessation of the draft in the early 1970s, were the motivating factors in me moving off base in Germany and onto "the economy." Soldiers who were not total screwups were authorized bachelor's quarters and "separate rations" allowances, which boosted a private's pay considerably but with commensurate risks. The extra dough was helpful, but the Deutschmark was strong then, so the exchange rate was fearsomely against you, and separate "rats" meant you couldn't eat at the mess hall. Sure, you could sneak in here and there and get over, but not routinely. The allowance allowed you to eat on the economy for a number of weeks until it was gone, your tab perilously high with a gasthaus' proprietor, and his once smiling face now a grim, thin-lipped physiognomy, right arm extended fingers and thumb rubbing together indicating: "Put some jack right here, Mack."

The only solution was "Off to the PX!" on payday for a sackful of groceries prompted by the mature decision to cook something or go hungry. That's easy: Cook something! Cereal, meat and potatoes, mustard, ketchup and mayo, Wonder® Bread, peanut butter, canned stuff like hash, soup, and B&M baked beans, pretzels, peanuts and chips, milk, juice, frozen corn, Coke. Plus beer and cartons of Marlboros in the box, although the latter two weren't "groceries," but "necessities."

The resulting menu was not too varied, but it was satisfactory. Some careful shopping, plus judicious black market sales of rationed cigarettes to the displaced Polish laborers in barracks next to the company area, ensured sufficient cash for an occasional night out with supplementary necessary food like pizza, snails, cannelloni, a house special salad, schnitzels of all sorts *und pommes frites*, plus *schaschlik*, sausages, and curry at the *Schnellimbiss*, a quick-stop snack bar.

One life-influencing discovery I made in the army was chili. The instruction that ensued made clear the importance of the substance, not just a food, but a food group all by itself. My roommate, Gregory P. Mills of Independence, Missouri, said in the course of putting together a shopping list:

"Put chili on there."

"What?"

"Put chili on there!"

"What's chilly?"

"What?"

"What's chilly!?"

"Not chilly, *chili*. You don't know what chili is? You've never had chili? Where the hell are you from? What's the matter with you? Are you stupid?"

"No. No. New Hampshire. Nothing. And no. We don't have that in Dover, and, in fact, I don't think we have that in New Hampshire. What is it?"

Chili, Mills explained (after rounds of laughter, derision, and disbelief), is meat and beans in a sauce. It's all-around food. You can eat it for breakfast, lunch, or supper. It's nutritious and wholesome, but, most importantly, it's filling. Some people make it, but you can get it out of the can, and it's good. Cowboys ate it, but everyone eats it now, and Kansas City is famous for chili (as he pronounced Kansas City famous and The Best for everything from barbecue, to women to industrial might, not too mention the Chiefs). You can put Tabasco on it and crumble crackers into it, he said, and it's even better. We got a can of chili, and from that date on, I felt like a real soldier: eating chili and putting Tabasco in it.

Thirty-five years later, my chili is decent.

Once out of the army towards the end of 1974, and working for the Veterans Administration in Togus, Maine, cooking played an incrementally more important role in my life than it did as a soldier. VA police work around the clock, so I was doing shift work. The annual salary of $7,596 per year for a GS-4 police officer wasn't huge money, but it beat the $2.50 an hour rate of $5,200 annually at the tannery in Dover. Plus the chance to return the family home to an empty nest for my parents forced them to compel me to take the job one hundred miles away. The Protective Section at Togus, consisting of a four-man crew of firefighters and usually one cop per shift, was a thrifty bunch. They had to be. Most of the firefighters had families and mortgages. Most also had second jobs and several had third jobs, so economy was paramount. They brought their lunch—sandwiches mostly and leftovers for supper—and they hunted for meat. Wives always had a hunting license and they got their deer tag filled. The firefighters didn't make a communal meal like the urban firehouses because of the expense and the work schedule of rounds and inspections and maintenance.

Cops worked an eight-hour shift, so I usually arranged to eat before work, mostly bachelor cooking: meat, pork chops, or chicken and potatoes and applesauce; an occasional steak; hamburger patty or spaghetti. Other times, I'd pack a sandwich and a piece of fruit. The coffeepot was always on in the Protective Section, and it was good coffee. Naturally, donuts were frequently around.

Geography, timing, and circumstances contributed to the next evolution of my cooking skills when I returned to college in Minnesota in early 1976. The Twin Cities has always been hip in its own Minnesotan way, and that era was no exception. Minnesotans, weirdos by their own admission, were doing interesting things with food. Commercially, there was fine dining at places like The Blue Horse, The Rosewood Room, and The Lexington. Neighborhood joints were serving up burgers and fries or steak and a baked potato and a house salad for $6, and innovations were occurring all over the metro area. St. Paul had a kitchen making "Chicago" style deep-dish pizza, while another pizzeria hawked genuine "New York style" pizzas. Fabulous, both of them. A rib joint opened up, serving real smoked spareribs. Downtown Minneapolis unveiled the New French Café, serving homemade croissants and baguettes, as well as French roast café au lait, and the line Saturday mornings sometimes went out the hallway door to Fourth Street. Bistros and ethnic and specialty restaurants flourished, while old standbys like El's Breakfast still served millions of waffles and bacon strips to Golden Gopher students nursing aching heads the day after. True gustatory innovation occurred when a Mexican restaurant opened in the high fashion St. Anthony Main development. Customers ranged from Control Data execs and their sleek women, to grungy students, to the occasional trio of Guadalajaran illegals, spending large for a nostalgic sample of their native Jaliscan cuisine.

My roommate, pursuing an advanced degree at Minnesota, was a great cook, unafraid to try something never before accomplished: following the instructions in a cookbook. I had seen women do this before. My mother and aunt used cookbooks, and an army nurse I knew in Germany did, too. The results were usually pretty good. I'd seen men use books as guides before—*Chilton's* for backyard auto repair and a naval engineer friend from the Portsmouth shipyard who learned to golf from the *Encyclopedia Britannica*. However, the Boss didn't use cookbooks, nor did SSG Carl Holcomb, mess chief in Germany, or at least that I ever saw.

But the creations turned out pretty well, and in looking over this new-found resource, I discovered plain directions offering basic information on how to make . . . anything. Whoa! Quality grub, too! Homemade bread or rolls. Casseroles. Different kinds of meat. Varieties of cakes and cookies other than yellow cake with chocolate frosting or Toll House cookies. Even ideas for non-skanky vegetables like stuffed peppers or sautéed mushrooms. New vistas indeed. Clever, too. Different cookbooks offered different instructions. Want to make genuine schnitzel? Get ahold of Betty Wason's *The Art of German Cooking*, which told you plainly how to do it. And better yet, the book told you how to make warm German potato salad, sauerbraten, rot salat, spaetzle, and rahmschnitzel, like the schnitzel factory at Kindsbach.

My roommate's graduate ed connection worked in favor of expanding comestible horizons, too, because she was working in the lab with bright people whose varied interests left them open to new experiences. As teaching assistants and lab workers, they were relatively poorly paid, so economy was important. A cookbook at $10 and $5 worth of specialty groceries could provide a meal for four—a new experience and a party on Saturday night, too.

For example, spicy Chinese cooking, "Satch-wan," was something just being talked about in newspaper food pages and with-it circles. A young faculty member, being well-read and adventurous, acquired a cookbook and began to experiment, and the results were so delectable he broadcast the news to all in the lab. One dish in *Mrs. Chiang's Szechwan Cookbook* he described as "fantastically delicious." That was sufficient prompting. We made a batch of the recommended Grand Duke's Chicken and Peanuts and Lord have mercy! A combination of marinated chicken, loads of garlic, green peppers stir fried, but still crispy, generous chunks of cayenne red pepper to dampen the brow, and fresh-cooked peanuts for taste, crunch, and texture made the dish accessible, foreign, hot, tasty, and spectacular. In other words, the scientist was right. It was fantastically delicious.

The cookbook was the funnel that helped bring together a trio of thoughts that had been independently coursing through my undergraduate mind: Eating is vital—and in order to eat, you've got to cook. That was a truth I confirmed in the army. Food does not prepare itself. You have to make the effort, because if you don't, you won't eat. But the commitment to cook bespeaks a number of unspecified demands. You have to take the time necessary to make the meal. You've got to have a minimum of tools: knives, cutting boards, utensils, pots and pans, soap, scrubbees, and sponges. You've also got to shop, since supplies don't provide themselves.

In a man's world, to "shop" is truly a four-letter word of the vilest sort. It universally evokes anxiety, even fear, in men, connoting as it does all the worst of women: poking around and poring over fabric and draperies, "dry goods," and "notions" (What the hell are they?); holding up dresses and blouses and air-comparison sizing. Female shopping also seems to work best with a pal who's sufficiently cognizant to recognize a "bargain" and who takes joy in finding just the right twenty-sixth pair of shoes. What a horrible waste of camaraderie when you could be engaging in truly important endeavors, such as "drinking," "watching football," or "playing poker."

Man grocery shopping is different. Man grocery shopping is the exercise of judicious authority and precision. No consulting. No compromise. No conversation. You get your cart; you buy what's on your list (and because it's your list, it might include "notions" like orange cream cupcakes and Devil Dogs, sweet butter, margarita mix, and Roquefort cheese, or "dry goods" like cashews, Starbucks French Roast coffee, and nacho cheese flavored Doritos, high end or low class as you see fit); you obtain the ingredients you need to make the meals you want; and all the while you stay alert for periodic episodes of "beauty," or merely "good-looking," childless and pushing a cart in the other direction.

Man grocery shopping is a useful pastime with occasional aesthetic gratifications. What's not to like about that?

Eating is fun. You're satisfying a fundamental need, benefaction at the most basic level. The enjoyment of eating is often enhanced when you're sharing a meal with someone, an acquaintance, a friend, or a lover. That situation is latent with pleasure too, good company, or interesting conversation, or just warm feelings stoked by warm food. Eating promotes a sense of intimacy that other fun undertakings don't: skiing or shooting guns or riding motorcycles or watching stock cars at the track or pro football players on TV.

When you're cooking, with about the same amount of effort, you can turn subsistence into delectation. Say you're hungry and you're making spaghetti and marinara sauce. You boil the spaghetti, open a jar of Classico® sauce, heat it, and put it on the cooked pasta. Mmmm. Eat and be satisfied.

But . . . suppose you opened also a small can of sliced mushrooms, drained them, and dumped them into the sauce, and shook a one-fourth teaspoon of hot pepper flakes into it to increase its piquancy. You next grabbed a head of romaine lettuce out of the fridge, ripped the tops off, rinsed them, dried them on paper towels, tore them apart, and threw them in a bowl. You sprinkled on a few croutons, some salt and pepper, and a palmful of grated Parmesan or Romano cheese and some bottled Caesar dressing. You next cut a slice of bread, buttered it, sprinkled on some garlic powder and grated Parmesan or Romano cheese, and slapped it into the toaster oven for four minutes, and opened a bottle of $8 Chianti Classico, and poured yourself a glass.

With literally a couple of can openings, a couple of jar top unscrewings, a cork removal, a rip and a toss here, a slice and a sprinkle there, and in the same amount of time as it took you to make subsistence grub, you've gone from basic to respectable nutritious repast.

The take-away lesson: With nearly the same amount of effort, you can elevate your diet from "bare" to "ample," not to mention "nutritious." Home-cooked food is good food and it's easy, way less expensive than eating out, and it is better for you since you control the ingredients and the freshness. There are some new skills to learn, but the fundamentals are quickly derived and can be put immediately to good and productive use.

"Give a man a fish and you feed him for a day. Teach a man to fish and you feed him for a lifetime," goes the Chinese proverb, and it's true. But the unsaid aspect is that unless that man is always going to eat sushi, then someone better figure out how to cook that fish. Then he and his family will be fed for a lifetime.

Oh, and speaking of Chinese, how seminal was Mrs. Chiang's cookbook? It was so central that twenty-five years later, deep in the winter in Connecticut with the snow lying gray and chill on the lawn and colds making everyone feel headachey and juicy and poor, a batch of Grand Duke's Chicken and Peanuts served as comfort food supper for adults and children alike, sends all to bed satisfied, warmth-restored and seriously garlicked-up, properly anticipating spice and red pepper diminishment of rhinovirus upon wakening the next day.

Think of it! Chinese stir fry as comfort food and therapy in middle-America Connecticut? That's seminal!

Grand Duke's Chicken with Peanuts

Ellen Schrecker and Mrs. Chiang state that the name of the Chinese gourmet who invented this dish is long lost to history, but they assert his taste was impeccable as witnessed by the finished product. The authors say they believe the dish to be precisely representative of Szechuan cookery, combining as it does a number of tastes, textures, and flavors to produce a perfect whole. "Fantastically delicious," in other words.

Preparation
½ cup fresh peanuts
If the peanuts have dark red skins on, dump them in a bowl and pour a cup of boiling water over them. Soak the peanuts for a few minutes then drain. Pinch the skins off.

1 whole boneless skinless chicken breast (about 1 pound)
Cut the meat into 1-inch cubes.

1 ⅓ tablespoons soy sauce
½ teaspoon granulated sugar
1 teaspoon sesame oil
1 teaspoon Chinese rice wine or cooking sherry
1 egg white
1 scant tablespoon cornstarch
Put the chicken pieces in a bowl and add the soy sauce, sugar, sesame oil, cooking sherry, and egg white. Mix and set aside.

2 green peppers or 3 large hot green peppers
Cut the peppers into 1-inch squares.

10 cloves garlic
Smash the garlic cloves with the flat of your knife, then peel. Chop the garlic into pieces about the size of a match head.

½ inch piece fresh ginger
Peel the ginger and mince it into slightly smaller pieces than the garlic.

5 dried red peppers
Break the red peppers into 4 pieces each.
2 scallions (chicken)
Clean the scallions, then chop both the green and white parts crosswise into ¼-inch pieces. Add the scallions to the chicken.

Cooking
3 tablespoons peanut oil
Heat your wok or pan for 15 seconds over a medium flame before pouring in the oil. The oil will be hot enough to cook with when the first tiny bubbles form and a few small wisps of smoke appear.
(peanuts)
Add the peanuts to the hot oil and stir fry them for 2 or 3 minutes using your cooking shovel or spoon in a scooping motion to swirl them around the pan so all are exposed to the hot oil. They cook fast, so watch out. As soon as the peanuts have started to turn golden brown, remove them from the pan.

(green peppers)
½ teaspoon salt
Add the green peppers to the oil in the bottom of the pan. Stir fry them for 30 seconds over a fairly high flame, then add the salt and continue to stir fry for another 45 seconds. Remove the peppers from of the pan.

¼ cup peanut oil
Remove the pan from the heat and wipe it out with paper towels. Return it to the stove and reheat over a fairly high flame for 15 seconds before pouring in the fresh oil.

(garlic, ginger, and dried red peppers)
When the oil is ready, add the garlic, ginger, and red peppers. (One way to test the oil is by floating a tiny piece of ginger in it. If the ginger sinks, the oil is too cold; if it turns brown immediately, it is too hot. The ginger should just float fizzling on the surface.) Cook the ginger, garlic, and red peppers for 20 seconds, stirring constantly.

REDNECK *Gravy*

(chicken and its marinade)
Then add the chicken and its marinade and stir fry for 1 minute.

(partially-cooked green peppers)
Return the green peppers to the pan and stir fry them together with the chicken for another minute.

1 tablespoon soy sauce
Add the soy sauce to the chicken and stir fry for about 15 seconds. The chicken is ready when it has stiffened and turned white.

(peanuts)
Finally, return the peanuts to the pan. Stir fry everything together for 30 seconds longer, then serve.

CHAPTER 3

Gettin' There

Getting offshore may have been trickier and more convoluted than it should have been. Louisiana offshore catering companies crave live bodies like medical schools crave dead bodies. They advertise in all the Louisiana and Texas newspapers, some Mississippi papers, and other places in the South where recruits may be found or the unwary may malinger.

Offshore is specialized work, and offshore catering is even more specialized. It is rigorous, demanding, and low-paid, which is why the catering companies advertise their jobs all over the world and seek workers where they can find them.

The companies will accommodate you, too, within reason. They're strict about being on time and at the place you're supposed to be, but a police record is no obstacle to employment; they'll make arrangements if you have a court date; and probation is a factor that needs to be worked around rather than being a deal-breaker.

So while a warm, somewhat sentient body is wanted, what isn't expected is a fifty-five -year-old former newspaperman and editor with catering experience thirty years ago, membership in the American Dietetic Association's Food and Culinary Professional group and numerous classes at the Connecticut Culinary Institute notwithstanding.

Catering companies are headquartered all around Louisiana, many in the cities most closely associated with offshore work: Lafayette, Houma, industrialized New Orleans, Harahan, and others. Finding the companies is easy in the computer age. Google "Louisiana offshore catering companies" and screen after screen pops up. The internet makes applying for them easier, too.

Taylors International Services, Inc. in Lafayette is the first to respond to my application. Lafayette is about sixty miles west of Baton Rouge, a straight shot on Interstate 10, over the 18.2-mile bridge across the Atchafalaya swamp, errr, ecosystem. The city is the heart of Cajun country as well as being the petroleum capitol of the state. The "Oil Center" office complex is downtown, the University of Louisiana Lafayette's reputation resides comfortably in its world-class petroleum engineering program, and oil, drilling, and oil-service companies people the city's business population.

The woman on the phone suggests I drive out Monday morning, fill out some additional paperwork, and talk to the human resources people. Fine. Early Monday finds me in Lafayette. My paperwork is misplaced, so I fill out the application again as well as additional paperwork.

John Taylor (not *the* Taylor of Taylors International), the human resources guy in charge of offshore, introduces himself and quizzes me.

"I see you've been an editor and, what's this, public affairs?" he says.

"Yes, public information officer. But I want to go offshore. I have catering experience."

"Hmmmm. Yes, thirty years ago."

"I'm a good cook. I want to have an offshore work experience and I know I can cook for a dozen or fourteen men. . . ."

"A dozen or fourteen men? Some of our rigs have sixty or seventy guys on them."

"Sixty or seventy men?" I shout. "I'm not good enough to do that right now."

"I know," he says, "which is why I won't send you out there alone. You need to make a couple of trips as a galley hand to get the lay of the land and see if this work is for you."

OK, I'll go as a galley hand. The objective is to get offshore as a cook, but if I get offshore, the chances of being a cook are greatly improved. And the truth is, I do need some refresher time in a subordinate position before assuming the checked pants of cook.

Working offshore on an oil rig can be dangerous. You're stranded somewhere in the middle of the ocean, on a tiny platform, usually miles from emergency services. Transportation to and from the rig is by crew boat or helicopter, the latter having its own particular perils.

Drilling for oil is inherently risky. Of course measures are taken to make that drilling as safe as possible, but the fact remains you're sticking a probe thousands of feet into the earth in hopes of striking oil, and you might just find it and have it come boiling back up those thousands of feet right at you. Gushers happen, despite best practices and precautions, with cataclysmic effect.

Beyond the possibility of blowback, workers are involved in labor in an industrial setting. The workspace is compressed; the equipment is heavy; and cranes are constantly in use, swinging unwieldy and weighty objects through the air. Physical toil takes a toll, but it's also easy to fall or trip, drop something on you or have something dropped on you, get jammed, clobbered or smashed, crushed, pinned or banged, dinged, wounded or thrashed, dumped, bumped or thumped or . . . you get the idea. All of these and more have occurred uncounted times in the oil business. It's a part of the landscape. The oil and drilling companies know this, and because accidents cost money and the object is to make money, not spend it, and especially *not* spend it on workers' compensation, the companies are extremely conscious of safety.

Constant safety is promoted through hiring practices and training, training, training. Hiring is the first line of defense and safety is promoted by extensive screening for medical conditions, physical fitness, and capability. Equally as important is screening for drug and alcohol use.

Naturally, the catering company comes in for its share of screening and safety dunning, and, of course, caterers are subject to nearly the same training and certification as the oil men. Once application paperwork has been completed and criminal justice system status has been ascertained and reconciled, the would-be caterer is off to the occupational medicine clinic for physical and urine test.

The clinic Taylors uses is just off Ambasador Caffrey Parkway in a part of Lafayette designed for entrepreneur franchisees of every stripe and their motorist patrons. The building looks small and heavily fortified. Appearances can be deceiving, but the building gives the impression of being hunkered down and willing to let go its occupational medicine secrets very reluctantly, if at all.

Nothing to fear on account of health or drugs, I confidently stroll in, announce my intentions, fill out the paperwork, and do not lie. The form advises that the clinic has methods of detecting medical untruths and non-compliance, and failure to be forthcoming can result in "termination." Given the universal finality of that advice and the battered functionality of the clinic (sort of like police court, county farm reception station, or the gulag), I play it safe and confess all: broken arm in 1956; split skull in 1957; childhood stitches; hockey wounds; army traumas; and every surgery of every inconsequentiality, including freeze-dried warts and ganglion cysts removed.

In moments I am summoned forth and essentially told to "git." Being a geezer of fifty-five years and looking to go offshore is questionable enough, but being a geezer who's had double bypass heart surgery, I don't even get beyond the initial paperwork. I explain that all's medically rationalized and the only physical limitation I have in the wake of the surgery is a moratorium on shoveling snow, which isn't likely to happen in Louisiana and is even less likely to be necessary offshore. The occupational medicine folks are polite but firm. I'm sent packing back to Baton Rouge with a demand for a medical waiver from my cardiologist—in Connecticut. That's OK. I'm not worried. My cardiologist is a pal and is accessible by e-mail. Forty-eight hours later, I've got my waiver. Then back to the clinic in Lafayette for more physicals. The docs in the clinic accept the waiver, but then decide that given the exigencies of the circumstances, a stress test is a better indicator of my overall health. I've had a stress test in the past, but not recently or within a year, so a new one is called for.

This is a serious setback. Recently transplanted from north to south, I'm new here and live in the city without a physician, cardiologist, dermatologist, dentist, chiropractor, podiatrist, ophthalmologist, nurse anesthetist, reiki master, hypnotherapist, massage therapist, or tai chi instructor. Compounding woes, I'm told Louisiana doesn't allow "self-referral," meaning you can't go into a clinic and say, "Hi. I'm Joe Blow and I'd like a cardiac stress test."

They're liable to respond (with customary Southern reticence) "Take a hike, pal."

Fortunately, I've got good health insurance coverage, which means the out-of-pocket expense will be covered. But it's plain I'm not going offshore any time soon. I need to obtain a primary care physician, get an appointment with her, obtain a referral to a cardiologist, make an appointment with him, and then schedule the stress test. By that time, my stress level will be so high that I'll probably need a series of electroshocks for manifestations of acute neurosis.

And with a little luck and a lot of good will, in just more than two weeks I've done all of it thanks to Betty Miller of Louisiana Cardiology Associates, Baton Rouge; Dr. Roslyn Tabor of Summa Family Medical Practice, Baton Rouge; and Dr. Denzel Moraes also of Lousiana Cardiology Associates. The docs in the clinic in Lafayette aren't quite positive about the test results, but Dr. Moraes assured them—with only a further twenty-four-hour delay—everything was reasonably normal and the prognosis was good.

Thus vetted, I'm allowed to continue on with my

physical from nearly three weeks ago, which includes the most carefully controlled and supervised urine test I've ever encountered, and a visit with a physician to visually check physical structure and mobility.

I've passed everything and am given paperwork to bring back to Taylors Department of Human Resources. The people in the office aren't as surprised to see me as they appear to be marginally uncomfortable. They sort of recognize me, but after nearly three weeks, it might be the discomfort of the sudden reappearance of the proverbial bad penny, or the reapparition of an old and disagreeable poltergeist. Taylors human resources people see everything. Like school teachers or cops each in their environments, there's not too much that can happen or can be said during the hiring process that the Taylors folk haven't seen. Applicants have the darndest circumstances that inhibit speedy completion of the process from real to hyperventilated: family woes or relationship issues or money questions or legal wrangles or mental burdens or physical uncertainties or spiritual reservations or personal involvements or inferred difficulties or imagined impedimenta. Applicants frequently disappear during the initial employment process when the full- or even the partial-import of what they're about to do sinks in, but they seldom reappear to continue the process weeks later. "Excuse me, I need to take a few weeks off to go on a bender before I continue with signing on for a job that pays minimum wage and will send me offshore for fifty percent of my life. Let's pick this up the end of the next month. See you then! Hey man, any chance of an advance on my salary!?"

So my paperwork is accepted, if unenthusiastically, and I'm scheduled for "back school" and water training the next day.

Back school and water training are two more safety and health-related initiatives. Back school aims at preserving your back, which is always at risk if you're impetuous or young and doing heavy labor in a non-thoughtful manner. Water training teaches you to survive should you find yourself in the drink.

In back school you're shown how not to blow out lumbar and spine with proper techniques of hoisting and lifting, going upstairs and down bearing a load, and the safest and best methods for toting things. The training classes also expand on other safe-work issues like demonstrating agility while using a safety harnesses on structures fifteen feet in the air, and observing and recording physical exertion of potential employees at heavy labor.

Proper training reduces accidents, but just as importantly, it may also limit worker's compensation liabilities, if, in the case of a dispute, the companies may truthfully state it was a worker engaging in unauthorized behavior that resulted in the injury.

Back school starts with a little quiz, a practical exam if you like, such as can you hang off a hawser, a three-inch thick piece of rope, for ten seconds without touching ground? The duration of the test more or less represents how long it would take to evacuate you and others from the rig by crane in the case of an emergency. Since I'm game, but old and impressionable (as opposed to young, strong, and stupid), the reality of the offshore experience so much sought after was brought home to me. I reflected on the route and method of descent and reckoned, "Nothing's going to go wrong, but if something does, you better have your shit together beaucoup, mister, or you could end up charred black and floating face down in the Gulf. Learn this stuff." My classmate, a poor thirty-eight-year-old, pear-shaped 340-pounder, gritted his teeth and struggled to stay aloft while gravity tugged relentlessly at his girth. My other classmate, a sixty-three-year-old chain-smoker from Tennessee who drove a '92 gray Cadillac hearse with a Tasmanian Devil license plate and needed a triple bypass but couldn't have it because the docs said it was just plain too risky, didn't do so hot escaping the rig.

I was surprised at the discomfort in hanging off that rope. When I was a kid I climbed trees and hung off ropes and branches and monkey bars without peer. Even in the army thirty years ago, the hand-over-hand stuff was so easy that I usually swung to every other bar like an orangutan. Hanging off that rope, doing something I hadn't done in thirty years, I realized things had changed. I was eighty pounds heavier, for instance. My hands were right atop one another, too close together, and my weight, plus the downward pressure from my top hand, actually crushed my bottom hand and it hurt and imperiled the grip. Hands farther apart next time was the lesson learned.

After the "quiz," I excelled as the "youngster" in the class because the other pair were such physical wrecks.

Class and activities started: We carried a toolbox 150 feet to the back wall and returned a couple of times; we loaded dollies with sandbag and concrete "groceries" and wheeled them around five times while Mr. Terrence, the back school instructor, watched how we lifted stuff and didn't allow us to "body torque;" we picked up and toted a half-concrete block up stairs and around the loop a couple of times and put it on a shelf and retrieved it from a bin while never "stooping" and rarely losing balance; and we always used the "trailing hand" method of staying connected to the banister while descending stairs.

While the caterers were maneuvering concrete groceries on dollies, the guys testing to be roustabouts really got hammered. They were slamming two thousand-pound oil rig dangerous things suspended from derricks onto perilous oil rig pipeline things; smashing twelve-pound hammers onto infernal oak chopping blocks at a brisk pace; and pushing diabolical concrete-block loaded wooden bins (without wheels) around concrete floors with nothing other than slave power. Periodically, they'd stop to take a drink of water, and the guzzling was like watching a camel replenish.

Much of their labor took place while they were attached to a heart monitor so that if the subject exceeded the limits and performance standards, they'd be out of there quicker than you could say, "Can I call my attorney?"

After training and show-and-tell classes, employees are tested to ensure the concepts are momentarily recalled, if not memorized. Passing the test earns certification that goes into your personnel jacket. What it most likely means is, "Upon certification, I agree to forever surrender my legal position to claim in a lawsuit I never learned or heard any of this."

Once back school is done and the attendees have been certified or returned to the street corner, there is a break for lunch and the afternoon is spent in the pool at water training. The official training is known as "water survival course." The Taylors info sheet informs participants the program calls for two pairs of trousers, "one pair you are wearing and an extra pair," shorts/swim trunks, and a beach towel. The info sheet does not address "skivvies" for the curious members of the class, but sometimes it's possible to think too much about things. If one needs two pairs of trousers, does he also need two pairs of skivvies, too, so that one will be "dry?" Well, no. The pair you are wearing is exchanged for swimming trunks/shorts and the pair of trousers you are carrying are made into life preservers after trapping some air in the legs and sticking your head between them to help you float away from the rig disaster that found you in the water in the first place.

Water safety training reviews initiatives such as survival with ad hoc flotation devices, drownproofing, communal/team survival, and escape from a simulated helicopter crash. Some of this stuff is pretty good. It's well thought out, practical, easy to learn, and has obvious utility. I'm one of the more fortunate participants because I can swim, a skill our mother insisted my sister and I learn at an early age. Many guys in the twelve-man class can't swim and no few are vocal about the water: They don't like it. I can't imagine the anxiety and fear of jumping into the deep end of the pool, life preserver or no, without being able to swim. But then again, I can't imagine not being able to swim. For those poor devils, it's going to be a long, tough afternoon.

The program starts with the least encumbered method of rig emergency evacuation—jumping off.

Jump instructions are always prefaced by an earnest sermon on the merits of *not* entering the water around a rig. The upshot is: Being in the water either alone or with company is the very worst situation offshore. If you're in the water, it means catastrophic calamity aboard the rig.

For whatever reasons, safety measures and evacuation procedures have failed and the situation aboard has deteriorated such that only immediate bailing out will preserve life. That's drastic. Just how drastic may be intimated from the fact most rigs are sixty to eighty feet above the water, many others are a lot higher than that, and a leap of that magnitude in itself threatens limb if not life. The instructors relay the best piece of advice: Look down before you jump; there might be a crew boat or an escape pod under you. If it's clear, then jump.

Jumpers practice wearing a life preserver, as you would while abandoning rig, standing at the deep end of the pool, looking down, announcing the coast is clear, grabbing the life preserver to keep arms tight against the body and crossing legs to protect the "groin area," as the TV football analysts say, and launching yourself. The water is seventy to seventy-two degrees, warm by Maine standards, but chilly by Louisiana lights, judging from the comments.

Drownproofing is next, an easy technique to learn—if you're not afraid of the water. Drownproofing consists of taking a breath of air and holding it, then relaxing face down in the water, arms hanging loosely, using the buoyancy of the air in your lungs to keep you floating. When you need air, kick your legs to bring your head out of the water, exhale, inhale, and then resume your floating posture.

I use drownproofing to rest when I'm swimming or floating in the water, and have for years. I can sympathize with the non-swimmers who are struggling to learn it though, because the idea of floating face down in the water is frightening, not too mention counterintuitive. Floating face down in the water and not breathing is a standard definition of drowning. The big difference between it and drownproofing is that in drownproofing you're consciously not breathing, while in drowning, you've unconsciously aspirated water and probably have breathed your last. Either way, it's an unnerving circumstance the instructors handle well, but no amount of coaching can displace the non-swimmers' terrors.

Making a personal floatation device out of the trousers you are not wearing is a handy stay-alive tip. Maneuvering your trousers off in the water is a useful skill the instructors don't require, but I did it anyhow. It's not exactly difficult, as it is tricky. You are immersed in the water, after all. Being able to hold your breath and go underwater helps because you may have to pull the pants off each leg; gravity doesn't work the same way in the water and shaking the leg won't necessarily make the trousers fall off. Once off, tie the end of the legs together in a knot. Zip up the fly and button the waist so the trousers are sealed and the waist provides an opening. Holding onto the waist to keep it open, swing the trousers over your head and bring the opening quickly down into the water. The idea here is to capture some air in the legs and trousers and block it in with water. Gather waist together, keep it underwater, and hold onto it to prevent the air from escaping. Stick your head between the inflated legs of the trousers, while clutching the closed waist to your front and you have a perfectly serviceable, ad hoc personal flotation device.

Escape from the helicopter is next. The "helicopter" consists of an aluminum tube frame with a seat and seatbelt housed within it and Styrofoam pontoons attached under the seat's arms to aid flotation. The trainees enter the frame, belt in, then the frame is tipped over so the victim goes underwater upside down. The exercise simulates unbuckling and exiting from a crashed helicopter.

Instruction to the class includes: When the frame is tipped over, hold your breath, unbuckle the seat belt, look to see which way the bubbles are floating, and make your way to the surface.

It sounds easy enough, but if water is a foreign and frightening element, then the simplest instruction becomes more like a command for personal annihilation. Take the first one: "When the frame is tipped over, hold your breath." The advice to "hold your breath" is dependant on a number of things that for a non-swimmer are perilous, life-hazardous, frightening, impossible to comprehend, and "Sheee-it!" Like "when the frame is tipped over."

Even the most non-forward-looking realizes when the frame is tipped over, "Man, I'm going to be upside down in the water strapped into this damn thing that ain't no helicopter, just a death machine."

The reality is worse, my good man. When you're tipped over, you get a smart shot of water up your nose. It stings. It's not debilitating, but it is uncomfortable. Take that, the first manifestation of drowning, couple it with the irrational phobias *and* the rational fears of the water-averse, and you've got a trial by ordeal worthy of the finest dungeon master.

Most of the time the exercise goes OK. Trainees flipped, unhitched, surfaced, coughing and spitting, rubbing eyes and cussin.' But one big old boy after being flipped panics, manages to get unbuckled, and, finding his feet on pool bottom, stands up and launches that frame right up and over him. It's an impressive feat of panic-driven strength that

probably earns him an asterisk in his employment record:
* Do not sit anywhere near this individual during a helicopter flight over water.

Our last exercise is communal flotation. That's where swimmers form a chain by swinging their legs around the hips of the guy in front of them, much like riders on a toboggan. Thus connected, swimmers find safety and improved flotation. But toboggans aren't big in Louisiana, so the idea of connecting to a man in this way is new, unusual, and morally questionable. Nervous laughter betrays naked nerves and the thinnest veneer of reticence separating rampant homosexuality and rape. But the instructors persevere, manage to get everyone connected, and after making the group paddle forward, then stop and paddle backwards, the filthy practice is now fun and guys start clowning around, splashing their buddies with huge armloads of water in the guise of "paddling."

After two hours in the water, even the hearty are chilled and many are goose-fleshed and blue-lipped, so the call to exit the pool is most welcome. The chill instantly evaporates stepping out into the Louisiana heat and humidity.

Class is over for the day. Orientation is tomorrow at 7:30 a.m. at the Taylors office.

The meeting is conducted by the safety officer, Mr. Christopher, the guy who led the water survival course. Other Taylors officials instruct a session or dispense and collect paperwork as their specialty requires: supply takes sizes for uniforms, payroll gathers deposit slips to initiate direct deposit. Safety also plays a large role in orientation. Mr. Christopher's videos address behavior and proper conduct aboard, safety in another way, because different rules apply offshore in the maritime rather than the civil setting. Offshore, the Coast Guard, a federal authority, is the law enforcement agency, and the take-away message is: Don't do anything that's going to put you in dutch with the Coast Guard. The unspoken message is: The Coast Guard operates under different principles than the police—sort of like martial law—and you really don't want to mess with them. Period.

Safety videos review procedures for boarding the rig via cargo net (a "Billy Pugh basket," named after the manufacturer), galley dos and don'ts, and helicopter entrance and egress. During one of the mid-afternoon sessions, I am summoned by an instructor and asked if I can help a classmate collect his gear and transport him to a departure point on the other side of town. "Sure," I reply, "but I'll miss the video on dispatching, and I won't know how to do it." Call the dispatcher, they say, and that's all.

We take my car because it's reliable, but more importantly, because I have one.

My classmate is Bob, a fellow my age or maybe younger, but he looks older. A native of Texas, Bob is returning there to go offshore from Houston or Galveston, his first time offshore in fifteen years. There's more going to this assignment than I know at first. I'm not just to transport Bob, I end up actively coaching Bob, cheerleading, and watching the clock so he makes his rendezvous and accomplishes all he needs to. He knows the address of the hotel, but he's not certain of the best way to get there, so I navigate downtown, making a couple of wrong turns, but we arrive eventually. He keeps a conversation going, but it's not really a conversation and more like Bob speaking thoughts out loud. I gather he's had some tough luck in those fifteen years since he was last offshore. One marriage with children went sour, he may have done hard time in Texas (that's implied, not overtly stated), and his current relationship with a younger woman seems treacherous, unstable, and frightening to me. He mentions police, social workers, and the courts—not the most welcome of cupids.

The hotel is the St. Joseph Shelter for Homeless Men, which adds to the insight. Bob is gone a little longer than it should take to collect the large gym bag and a couple of plastic bags he exits with. On settling back into the car for our next stop, he explains there was some paperwork he needed to fill out that would send his check to the shelter. They'll hold it for him until he returns.

Our next stop is the cigarette store. He has a certain one in mind and that's easy to accommodate. It's within wandering distance of the shelter, a couple of streets over, and this store is designed to withstand a Cat 5 hurricane, an F-5 tornado, or a standard Quds force militia intent on jihad against a carton of Kools. Even if you successfully broke in, odds are slim you'd be able to break out unscathed. Bob emerges with a value pack of Salems—buy two, get one free—which means he has sixty cigarettes for fifteen or sixteen days, if he gets to his departure point tomorrow or the next day, for the fourteen days of the hitch.

He's already smoked two in the twenty minutes we've been in the car.

He fumbles with the value pack, not able to get it

open expeditiously. He chuckles and admits to being nervous. He hasn't done anything like this in a long time, he says.

Indeed!

"Listen, you're doing pretty good," I say. "You've got a job. You can do the job; you've been offshore before. You're squared away on money; it will be at St. Joe's when you get back. The hitch is only two weeks. If you don't like it, you can do something else. If you do like it, you can stick with it or maybe cook. Probably get a regular rig after a couple of trips. More money then, y'know?

"You're all set with getting to the departure point. You have a bus ticket to Houston and where you need to be, so what's to be nervous about? It's just different. The bus takes off at 5:10. It's now 4:45, and I'll have you there in ten minutes.

"You're doing good."

The bus stop turns out to be the parking lot of the discount liquor and tobacco retail warehouse at the intersection of I-10 and Ambassador Caffery Parkway. I don't think it's the most judicious hang-around place for a fellow in Bob's state of anxiety.

I watch his stuff while he goes inside to ascertain that this is the place the Houston bus stops. The clerk affirms it is. He comes out. I ask him if he wants me to stay until the bus arrives and he says no. I'm glad. I give him $10 and wish him "Bon voyage!" and shake his hand. It's trembling. Poor bastard. Hope it works out for him, but I'm afraid it won't. His past may be too checkered, his history too spotted, to think a galley hand job at minimum wage for a fifty-five-year-old, ex-con resident of a shelter will make a difference.

But maybe, with the grace of God . . .

I don't return to the office since it's late, instead turning the car east on I-10 towards home. I need a drink. I get my own assignment tomorrow, midmorning.

From e-mail:

Headin' out
Wednesday, February 14, 2007
8:14:08 p.m.

From: "Patrick Keefe"
To: The Boyz

That's right kiddies, your old Pappy is off to "Hercules 20" tomorrow morning at 3:00 a.m. out of Martin Terminal, Port Fourchon, Lou'siana aboard the Motor/Vessel Lisa.

Job title: Galley hand.

The "hitch" is for fourteen days, which if I understand it correctly, means I'm back March first—oh, in the family legend. Is it in like a lion or in like a lamb?

Considering we board and debark hanging onto a cargo net hoisted by a crane two hundred feet overhead, let's hope it's in like a lamb.

Hot diggity and Hoo-wah!

See y'all later.

Red Beans and Rice

In racketing around Lafayette, from Taylors to the clinic and back, I saw this restaurant, T-Coons, two blocks around the corner from the office at the intersection of Kaliste Saloom Road and West Pinhook Drive. The place looked interesting and there were usually cars about, so I stopped in. I'm glad I did. The restaurant was cafeteria-style Cajun—fried chicken, shrimp dishes, red beans and rice, rabbit, smothered pork or beef, plus daily specials. I had a plate of red beans and rice, a side of cole slaw, a dinner roll, and a soda, and the red beans were the best I'd ever had to that point. Even after a year offshore with a variety of good cooks and red beans every Monday, and a couple years eating Cajun food in Baton Rouge and south Louisiana, T-Coons' red beans still hold up in the top three.

My recipe differs from theirs as far as I can tell, chiefly in that they use hot Cajun sausage while I use a smoked ham shank.

Some recipes call for the beans to soak overnight. Other recipes proclaim soaking them or adding a pinch or two of baking soda will reduce flatulence associated with the beans. Perhaps. But on the rig, like in the boys' locker room or around the campfire in the Mel Brooks movie *Blazing Saddles*, flatulence isn't a problem as much as it's a competitive opportunity. Men, y'know?

I usually soak beans intended for baking, but not ordinarily red beans. On the rig, you make them on shift to serve at the next meal and there's no time for overnight deployment.

1 pound dry red kidney beans
1 green pepper, diced
1 yellow or white onion, diced
1 ham hock
2 cloves garlic, smashed
1 teaspoon Tony Chachere's
1 teaspoon dried thyme
½ teaspoon black pepper
½ teaspoon cayenne pepper
2 bay leaves

salt
4 tablespoons olive oil
2 quarts water

Dump beans in a colander and pick over carefully for stones or rubbish. Heat pot on medium and add olive oil. Toss in green pepper, onion, garlic, and spices and sauté until wilted. Add the ham hock, pour in the beans, and add water until it covers what's in the pot. Bring to a boil, then turn down to a simmer. Stir occasionally and cook for about two hours. Taste after an hour. Adjust seasonings until you achieve deliciousness. If you think it needs something, like more black or red pepper, or an ingredient you didn't add, like Worcestershire or jalapeno, go for it. Taste it and get it right. Remember this is rig cookery, and you can't do too much wrong. Before serving, mash maybe one-third of the mixture to thicken the plot. Serve over rig rice and offer up the Tobasco or Louisiana Hot Sauce.

CHAPTER 4

The Bidness

Going offshore isn't fun. It's demanding work. The hours are long. The job is physically tough, mentally challenging, and the setting is primitive. You are away from your family and your home for weeks on end. Your pleasures are severely curtailed. You may smoke or dip snoose, but you may not drink hooch, slug beer, smoke pot, indulge in recreational drugs, have sex. You work, eat, maybe watch some occasional TV, and sleep. For this you are paid well. Roustabouts, oil field laborers at the bottom of the salary pyramid, make in excess of $1,500 a week. Skilled workers earn more, and engineers and bosses earn considerably more. For half a year offshore, (2,184 hours, representing thirteen two-week hitches at eighty-four hours a week compared to the average work year of approximately two thousand hours) a roustabout can earn $35,000 to $45,000, and the pay scale goes up from there. Most of the men are devoted family men and are happy to make the sacrifice of working offshore, believing as they do, that their family's comfort is worth it.

To make things aboard the rig as palatable as possible, oil workers' basic needs are met by catering companies. Caterers contract with the oil or drilling companies running the rig to operate the galley and cook and serve the food. Caterers also provide hospitality services to the men: room cleaning and maintenance, laundry and maintenance of living quarters, and janitorial services.

There are three broad classes of catering jobs: cooks; galley hands (dish washers and kitchen help); and utility hands (bedroom and washroom attendant, launderer).

Catering personnel do less well in the salary department. You start at minimum wage, $5.15 in Louisiana at the time I started. Even that adds up when you consider the eighty-four hour week. But compare the approximate twenty-six-week earnings of $14,200 of a minimum wage galley hand to the $45,000 earnings of a roustabout, and the economic reality is apparent: Catering is a hard job that pays lousy. For the bold, for the forward looking, the persevering, and the hard worker, it's possible to make a living catering offshore. Some stewards, the bosses of the catering team, make six-figure salaries, and head cooks can make as much as notable chefs, but those are exceptions and the results of decades of effort. The practical reality is you can make $30 thou a year, but you'll work more than you'll recreate and you won't live large.

The skill requirement on the catering team drops off acutely after cook/steward. So does the desirability of the job. Galley and utility hands are not demanding jobs, but they are important jobs and can make a body raise a sweat if done right. The inclination to do the job right is a personal factor that can go either way. If you're conscientious, you'll likely work hard, need little instruction and less supervision, and do your job in addition to whatever else needs to be done. If, like Poke Salad Annie's daddy, you're a "lazy, no 'count," you'll need constant supervision and coaching and instruction and attention before you get fired or "run off."

Truthfully, the incentive to do the job right is diminished by the pay scale, which is atrocious. Considering how to improve your salary requires one to be able to reflect on something. That thought process bristles with sharp edges and harmful realities and pre-supposes the applicant *can* or *wants* to engage in extended thought. The possibility of making more money exists, but there is disincentive. That comes in the guise of the activity called "work."

Work, like thought for some folks, is a necessary evil yet intrinsic to the human condition. When Adam let Eve, in the now disreputable parable explaining why life can be crappy, fast talk him into something he hadn't thought about and didn't want to do, the Ur-"Honey-do" item, the Garden of Eden was transformed into "Earth," the peculiar and occasionally nasty place we inhabit today. "Original sin" was the broad-brush explanation of why sloth, envy, and lust were now considered "sins," where before as one wag put it, they were "The Job." Italy, a country of beautiful people, delicious food, and fantastical landscapes, was created and became a place both hellishly expensive and impossible to get anything done. Nordstroms appeared, where handbags still cost $500 for non-trophy wives whose hubbys only earned $500 every other week. And a World War II M-1 Garand, one of 14.4 gazillion manufactured, now cost five hundred times its original government price, if you can find one.

"Work outside the home for pay," more than a feminist descriptor, was now a requirement to live.

If you've never done it, work can be stressful. Work may be democratizing, but it is not democratic. Work is basically hierarchical, someone at the top telling someone at a subordinate level what to do. The someone being told is expected to do it. In exchange, the person doing the telling provides something of value. For example, in a law firm, the senior partners tell the junior partners what to do. The junior partners do research, write and file briefs, beat the bushes, and chase ambulances for clients, and amass billable hours. In exchange for this, the senior partners give the junior partners sufficient salary so they can afford a loft or mid-town condo, a trophy wife, and a BMW. There may be incentives, too, so that the junior partner with the most billable hours for the year earns a BMW at Christmas or is fast-tracked to become a senior partner his-own-self, where his rewards are commensurately greater.

In a prison, the work situation shares some characteristics with the law firm. In fact, in solitary confinement, the inmates research, write, and file briefs just like junior legal partners. Except there, they're doing it for their own selves and to gum up the legal system, instead of like lawyers, gumming up the legal system for a client and for money. Beyond the special circumstances of solitary, however, some factors change. For prison guards and administration, the motivators are similar to those in the law office: their labor in exchange for salary, benefits, and perks like tax-free cash for selling their charges cigarettes, garlic, pasta, and heroin, and arranging weekend "compassionate" passes to Las Vegas. For the inmates, the motivators are different.

They exchange their labor for food and bedding and to avoid having double-ought buckshot propelled into their physical being by guards riled-up over the refusal or reluctance of the inmates to perform labor for food and bedding.

An offshore oil rig shares some work characteristics of both the law office and the prison. Theoretically, the work situation is voluntary, like the law office. Practically, the reality is once you're out there, you're out there, like the prison: isolated, captive, alone, assigned to sleep two to a room, or if you're a roustabout, more likely six!

The job of the offshore caterer shares these liabilities and has a few peculiarities all its own to top off its undesirability. The pay is poor. The hours are long. The work is unskilled. You're the low man on the rig social scale; the knacker of the wagon train; the least acceptable caste, "Shudra," in a world of Brahmins and Ksyatriyas; the dung hand on the *corpus offshorosis*.

Given these constraints, it's plain to see that a certain person is required for the catering business. The person could be ambitious and forward looking, willing to take a stick in the eye short term for the possibility and indeed likelihood of promotion and betterment later, if he can tough it out. A galley hand, for instance, working to become a cook or a night cook/baker looking to become a steward. Or the person could be hard-working, but destined by language skills and immigration status to entry-level, minimum wage jobs. Or the person could be of limited skill and capability, the work being appropriate and meaningful for their God-given talents and capacities. Or the person could be unambitious but durable, willing, or encouraged by warrants and gang fatwa to leave home for a couple of weeks to do some laundry, make up a few beds, clean the crappers occasionally, and hold down the kind of job where more presence is required than effort. For this guy, catering—utility hand in particular—is just the job.

One utility hand described his philosophy on the night he arrived, which was also not-so-coincidently the night just before he was run off. "This job is all about money," he said, settling down in the TV room, remote in hand in the middle of his shift. "Money for nothing, that's what I'm into." Unfortunately, his plan on that rig didn't bear fruit when his behavior earned him a trip back to the dock on the morning boat even before his first shift was done. His point of view does not represent the philosophy or work credo of many, but it does represent some.

There's an ethnic component to catering offshore as well as historical antecedents. In the South, black folks cook. Always have and probably always will. Uncle Ben presenting that instant rice is a steward. Frank L. White dishing up hot Cream of Wheat, as "Rastus," is a chef. Aunt Jemima flipping those flapjacks is a cook.

On the offshore rigs, many stewards and cooks and catering hands are black. The commonality of race provides an immediate entrée offshore in the galley. Beyond the bond of race, the bond of the shared experience provides a more immediate, satisfying, and intense rapport.

Like seaweed innocently waving in the tide, merely biding its time before an ignorant sardine unwarily brushes by and the idyllic tendrils morph into flesh-rending sinews with fangs, or sorority sisters antennae on alert, now erect with delight upon discovering their mutually favorite boutique in Charleston is Miostile, similar levels of shared experience await exploitation for the guys. Each one revealed adds a building block to the structure leading irrevocably to the ultimate relationship: bro'hood. Think of the possibilities. In fact, one chance meet aboard rig yielded a homecoming of sorts: Bogalusa. Better yet, public housing in Bogalusa, a block down from Market Street and Central School. Even better still, mutual acquaintance and intimate knowledge of Sunny Wilson and her baby sister, LaReezha. With these accomplishments in common, little wonder you feel inclined to pronounce the newly met your "brother."

As Linc, the back guy on Mod Squad, might opine, "Solid!"

These social interactions and conventions weren't available to me. In fact, I caused curiosity.

On my first rig, after my first shift and back in the galley for supper, the nightside galley hand looked me over—pink face, green eyes, gray hair trimmed in a geezer-like manner, khaki Dickies, L.L. Bean work shirt (with no identifying externals)—and said, "Man, wha' choo doin' out here? You don't belong out here!"

I didn't know exactly what he meant. What? Too old? Too middle class? Too white? I didn't take offense, nor do I think he was being insulting. I think he was genuinely curious and perhaps just a tad annoyed that a guy like me would be working in the galley and, not so incidentally, taking a possible job from a brother.

"Offshore catering companies," a camp boss on a big rig I worked on would proclaim, "are thieves, connivers, and robbers." That was easy for him to say, he'd been

71

working offshore in between stints at restaurants for more than twenty years, and his black book held the name of every caterer, oil, drilling, and water transport company with a food service director and a lifetime's collection of stewards, chefs, and cooks he'd worked with offshore from Florida to Mexico.

With experience nowhere near as broad as his, I'd be reluctant to ascribe those epithets to all catering companies, but I can unequivocally say the companies are out to maximize their profit in a manner you don't normally apprehend these days. Greedy? Well that may be a little harsh—but only a little. Grudging? Yes. Definitely grudging. Grasping? Well, let's just say you don't want to get caught between them and the night deposit vault at the bank.

In the companies' defense, they find themselves in the odd position of having to make money the old fashioned way: by working for it. Unlike politicians who have money thrown at them during the campaign season and who subsequently just allocate what they want; or the government, which confiscates your money and gives it to someone else, extracting only a percentage handling fee to pay off high-priced unionized gummint salaries, benefits, and perks; or not-for-profits, depending upon monopoly, taxpayer largesse, or charity; for profit companies—small businesses in particular—are at the ass-end of the daisy chain, doing all the scut work to make the machine go. They need to offer a product with utility they can sell in hopes of making a profit. To do that they have to meet in the marketplace and defeat the other cut-throat sumbitch catering companies also snapping and yawping and scrapping after contracts like mudhounds after muskrats in a creek side lair.

Small business today faces such impedimentia that if the money wasn't so important, I'm sure they'd rather do something else. Catering is the worst of all worlds. The usual obstructions and flim-flam exist, along with the added dementia of food service, and its attendant dos and don'ts, quirky personnel, and regulation, working in a setting of drilling for oil offshore, a scary undertaking in a dangerous and hostile environment.

Careful planning, guile, and a host of factors must drop into line before profits come spouting out the end of the catering company worksheet. First off, you need an infrastructure to house, collect, train, certify, guide, and process your recruits. You need a human resources guy so the paperwork is right and the state and feds are quiescent. You need a safety guy to train and certify the recruits for offshore. You need a phone answerer to keep the curious and the meddlesome off your back; a supply technician to obtain uniforms and perform other esoterica; a clerk to help paddle up the crap creek you've chosen as a business venture; and two if not three dispatchers to cover all assignments all the time and to blame when things go awful.

Moreover, you need two or three guys of varying reputation and skill level to work with the knuckleheads you've hired and plan to send offshore. One home office guy will check out the stewards, cooks, and utility hands going drilling, another will work with the stewards, cooks, and utility hands going to a production platform, and the third guy will know just enough about both operations so you can send him off to troubleshoot tempestuous sites that are sure to occur.

That's ten full-time employees of varying salaries,

plus you, plus an office. And you haven't contracted with an occupational medicine shop to run your whizz tests yet, a best-practices safety and water training company to get your knuckleheads certified, and you haven't dropped a dime on insurance, workmen's comp, or the other myriad extortionate government-based obstacles between you and the rainbow.

Oh yeah, you also don't have any clients or offshore employees.

See where this is going?

It gets worse!

OK, so you promise, wheedle, cajole, fib, and lie your way into a contract with a drilling company. Now you've got to get the poor souls to go offshore. Where are you going to find them?

Right. Among the unemployed. Because if they were working, chances are they wouldn't be looking to go offshore.

There could be some few who were working and looking to change their circumstances. One Taylors applicant was a former Wal-Mart employee who had trouble with his boss and quit to escape being the fall guy for management derangement, or so he said. Another guy was a chain restaurant's manager-trainee-turned-drug-dealer who quit the business and needed to make himself scarce when the heat became oppressive. Another guy was a demolition laborer—not explosives, but crowbar and sledgehammer specialist. Yet another guy, in his early sixties, after thirty-five years of hitchhiking and squatting in cities across the U.S.A., eventually found a steady job as galley hand offshore to support himself and his pregnant sixteen-year-old girlfriend.

But by and large, who's unemployed? The weak, lame, and lazy, naturally. Other broad-brush groups include the young, the inexperienced, and underachievers. For the latter, offshore catering has something for each of them! For a yout', catering offshore offers a couple of entry-level jobs: galley hand and utility hand. Neither requires specialized skills. The work is easily learned in both cases. The same holds true for someone who wants to work but lacks experience. Of course "wanting" to work makes all the difference. Wanting to work is one of the magic motivators that will prompt a utility hand to clean the sinks or Windex the mirrors even as his laundry is caught up. Or will prompt the galley hand unbidden to clean the condiment trays and wipe down the condiment jars. For someone who's merely inexperienced and wants to work, offshore catering is a boffo way to jumpstart a career.

For the underachiever, offshore catering could be a godsend. And over a couple of decades, it can turn into a tolerable, if unfulfilling, career. The work is not too hard. You can do just the minimum and get along. You may not excel, but underachievers by definition fail to excel. Being offshore also eliminates temporarily at least much of the land-based hassle of life: demanding and hyper-critical family and in-laws; importuning wives, ex-wives, baby-mothers, and former girlfriends; infernal prosecutors, relentless detectives, and unforgiving probation officers; the landlord, rent collectors, and repo men; murderous gang-bangers, money-mad bond agents, shark-eyed loan enforcers. True, the pay is not too good, but if you're out there a lot, there's nothing to spend it on anyways, so what's the diff? And while you are out there, you eat well, sleep comfortably, work a little, and get some quality TV time. For an underachiever, this sounds like a description of paradise, without the seventy-two virgins, of course.

Where to find these individuals to fill out your staff? In the olden days, you could pay the sheriff fifty cents or a dollar per head bounty for each overnight guest he remanded into your custody, errr, employment. Today, of course, things don't work like that. Although, in Louisiana, it still couldn't hurt to drop a C-note into the local judge's re-election till with your business card attached. Otherwise you find the mugs, well, pretty much wherever you can roust them. You surely strike up a relationship with the local unemployment agency. You attend job fairs. If you're far sighted, you hustle career counselors at tech high schools and introduce your company to cooks teaching at low-end training centers or junior colleges.

It wouldn't hurt to become pals with, or at least an acquaintance of, parish probation officers either. While a recidivist could be trouble, a first-time offender realizing the seriousness and the nearly inescapable downward trend of his situation if not amended, might be eager to go away for pay to deflect the otherwise assuredly tragic trajectory.

You advertise in big-city newspapers where candidates' family members might possibly spot the ads and point them out to the candidates themselves. If you're truly diabolical and bold or cavalier in the face of potentially ruinous fines, you might advertise in Spanish language publications in Texas where recent immigrants, or newly-arrived-non-documented-yet-to-be naturalized-English-as-second-language workers might see it and take up your offer to escape offshore before they get deported.

You grab them all and don't ask any more questions than necessary. Remember, you're in a marginal position in your start-up company and the most important thing is to get working. All the trillionaires report that making the first billion is the hardest, and in your case, the first contract is the hardest. To make sure it goes right, you should send out one of your supervisors and have the other concentrate on securing a relief crew. Then everyone should concentrate on hustling contracts and building the stable of talent—or at least warm bodies.

Thus fully staffed, you set out to make some money (or recoup some of the money you never had but spent anyway trying to make a go of this offshore catering thang).

So the initial outlay and the work involved and the agita encountered are considerable, but, like drilling for oil, when you finally find some, it's damn sure worthwhile. Same in offshore catering. The economics are motivational. Caterers charge the drill companies per hour per man. They pay the same way, but the joy of owning a catering company comes from the difference in what they're paid versus what they pay you. Drill rigs pay caterers $20 an hour for a galley or utility hand; $28 to $35 an hour for a night cook or baker; and $38 or $40 for a day cook or steward. Galley hands start at $5.15 and can make as much as $8 after completing probation and demonstrating their aptitude and willingness to do the job. It's possible to make more, and of the tens of thousands of galley hands offshore, probably a handful are doing OK. I didn't meet too many—one or possibly two—but most of my acquaintances in the job were short-termers, new guys, or workers there temporarily before something (anything!) else came along.

New night cooks/bakers on a drill rig start at $8 per hour. The scale falls slightly on a production rig to $7.75 per hour because there the operative concept is: You're going to get your hours anyway, so why pay you more when you're going to be paid for hours you probably didn't work? Occasionally on larger rigs, for a variety of reasons—labor contracts that set minimum wages company-wide, custom, or tradition, or, however unlikely, social conscience—caterers' salaries are supplemented by the rig owner or main contractor. The additional money doesn't increase the caterer's cost, but it does redound beneficially to the cook. Usually, but not always. When the camp boss labeled all caterers worse than "gypsies, tramps, and thieves," he might've been speaking of the company one cook talked about that found the lure of an easy dollar simply irresistible.

This cook was working on a production rig and had been there for a number of months. He liked the gang and they liked him and his cooking. An opportunity came along to go to another rig and he was considering it. A new place would keep you fresh and change is good. He mentioned this to some of his pals and they mentioned it to the rig boss. The boss wanted to keep his men happy and retain his cook on board, so he asked the cook if some supplemental salary would keep things as they were and suggested two dollars an hour. Flattered, the cook agreed and the boss said he'd arrange it. The drilling company would pay the supplement through the catering company.

Several pay periods later, the cook noticed an increase in his pay, but the pay stub showed the increase to be a dollar an hour. The cook called catering HQ to find out what was happening, and the payroll clerk told him the company had decided the cook deserved a dollar an hour raise. "Wow!" thought the cook, "that means three bucks an hour." He told the clerk the drill company had given him a raise, too, and he was looking for that to come in on his pay. The clerk replied that he didn't know anything about that. After the next pay stub still showed the dollar raise, the cook asked the drilling boss if he ever managed to get the suggested raise approved. "Did that a month or so ago," the boss said.

A little more digging around and several increasingly angry phone calls later, with some strategic external pressure from the drill company, the cook had the situation scoped: the dollar raise was one-half the amount the drill company had contributed.

No possibility for "mistake" here; an "error" on the part of some naïve bookkeeper; or an accounting "glitch" due to complicated regulations or complex financial transactions. No chance of uncertainty over bracket creep, withholding requirements, or the tax implications of deferred compensation. This was just plain shysterism until the drilling company, which put up the extra dough, began stomping around and grousing, "What th' hell, y'know?"

The concept of reducing the salary for production catering crews "because you get your hours anyway" is a fine example of catering economics in that I don't exactly know how it works. I think it's basically postulated on thievery and effected by connivance. Although who are the thieves and who are the connivers is a toss-up. I don't lack certitude, and I've worked on two production rigs. As far as I know, in both examples, I got paid for when I worked. I know better than to unequivocally state there was no charging for hours I didn't work. I don't remember. I do remember long hours at work for a minimum salary and doing a conscientious job. So if there was some featherbedding, well, good for me!

Why the concept is elusive is illustrated below in an excerpt of a conversation with a dispatcher:

"There's a cook's job open on a platform in Lake Barre."

"Where's that?"

"Muzhiwuzhiah"

"Cocodrie, yeah. What's the pay?

"$7.75."

"No! Cripes, I was making $8 on Herc 21."

"Yeah but this is a platform, you're going to get your hours anyway."

"Hunh?"

Production platform catering crews work long hours. An offshore production rig shares some similarities with a drill rig in that it's self-contained, stand-alone, and the men are aboard for a shift of a certain duration. But unlike a drill rig, it collects, processes, and in some cases stores crude oil that has been extracted from the wellhead deep below. Some offshore platforms are equipped to both drill for and produce crude. These are formidable installations in terms of capital investment, size, and numbers of men aboard, but I didn't serve on one of those in the Gulf. The first production rig I was on, Apache South Pass 65, was in the middle of a refit from the effects of Hurricane Ivan in 2003. The platform had been shut down for a number of years and a construction crew of forty to forty-five was aboard making repairs, installing new equipment and bringing the facility up to date. The other platform, on Lake Barre, had been there for decades, patiently churning out product. The site was staffed according to the company's needs, generally with a four- or five-man crew, yet it periodically served as bunkhouse and chow hall for workers on projects nearby.

On SP 65, the construction crew worked thirteen to fourteen hours a day. The caterers worked longer.

The steward, Arthur, would get up at 2:45 or 3:00 a.m. to get going at 3:00 or 3:15 a.m. He'd check the galley, make coffee and grab a cup and smoke until the caffeine and nicotine started his heart and his eyes were a semblance of open rather than mere slits.

The catering crew was small: one cook/steward, one galley hand, and one utility hand. The hands would get up at 3:45 a.m. to get on deck around 4:00 a.m. When they arrived, the first thing to do was check the laundry and try to sort out the stuff the men had put in before turning in. Things got interesting when pals doubled up on laundry to save water (always a good idea offshore, and necessary on SP 65) and both were of similar size. If one big ole boy welder hitched up with a skinny little rigger, you could figure things out pretty easily. If not, and the duds were the same size, best just to fold it all and put in on the shelf, waiting for the owners to sort it out. After all, they're the ones who combined forces!

The hands would awaken the men at 5:00 a.m. by going through the rooms announcing it was 5:00 a.m., and turning on the lights. That gave the men an hour to get up, wake up, and get breakfast. Safety meeting was at 6:00 a.m., with attendance mandatory for caterers too. Safety meeting previewed the work for the day, which gang would be doing what, and reviewed safety concerns. The meeting lasted twenty to thirty minutes and the men went to work afterwards.

Arthur released me from my duties as galley hand to act as a utility hand in the mornings after breakfast to help make up rooms and catch up on laundry. Once that was done, I'd return to the galley to help out there. Laundry could take hours. Periodically, I'd return to the buildings I was responsible for to change loads, fold stuff, and return the dried articles to the rooms.

The evening meal was served at 5:00 p.m. and was over at 6:00 p.m. The utility hand pitched in with breaking down and cleaning up because Arthur liked to get us out the door at 6:30 p.m. Occasionally there was enough to do to keep us going until later, but mostly it was 4:00 a.m. to 6:30 or 7:00 p.m. That's fourteen and a half or fifteen hours, and I believe that's what we were paid for. Maybe that's what's meant by "getting your hours anyway," the difference between the twelve hours on the drill rig and the more-than-twelve-hours on the production platform. All the more reason to drop the salary!

I do not have a recollection of padding the time sheet. But if I did, I'm glad.

Biscuits and Gravy

This hearty breakfast combination arose from the time it was necessary to head outdoors, often before first light, and start working—everything requiring physical effort, from tussling with cows, to maneuvering cantankerous mule-powered plows and machinery, to bending and twisting, hefting and toting, stooping and squatting, and every darn thing a-raising sweat. It's still an appropriate breakfast item for men on a rig engaged in rigorous toil. It's a little less appropriate for today's urban and urbane warrior, heading off to the office or the cubicle farm to compute, e-mail, Twitter, talk on the phone, and instant message, and, generally, fly a desk. Why? Because biscuits and gravy for breakfast is a serious grub load. One web site pronounces one biscuit, halved, with gravy, represents 530 calories, with 310 of them coming from fat. That's about a quarter of approximately 2,200 calorie recommended daily allowance.

I love biscuits and gravy and I enjoy making it. I rarely eat it. And when I do, I usually take tiny portions just because it's such a gut buster. But sometimes that's just what's called for.

There are two recipes for biscuits. One is from biscuit mix, and the other is from scratch. Mix was most common the rigs. But occasionally I had to make them from scratch, and they always turned out decent, too.

From mix:
2 cups mix
Approximately ¾ cup milk
1 to 2 tablespoons melted butter

Preheat oven to 425 degrees. Pour mix into bowl and add milk slowly. Dough is ready when it's just barely moist. If there are dry clumps, good! Turn out dough onto a well-floured board. Pat into a square. Loosen square with a dough knife or spatula, fold over, and pat into a square three more times ending with a square 1½ inches thick. Flour dough and tools as needed to keep from sticking, but don't go crazy. Cut out biscuit-sized rounds using an empty soup can or drinking glass. Line baking sheet with parchment paper. If you don't have it, just place them on an ungreased baking sheet and add parchment paper to your grocery list for next time. Position rounds on baking sheet so that edges are just barely touching. Press thumb lightly on top of each biscuit, just enough to make an indent.* Bake 10 to12 minutes until golden brown, and start watching closely at 10 minutes. Brush tops with melted butter after done baking.

    * Making the sides touch yields soft-sided biscuits. If you prefer crispy sides, place them about an inch apart on the baking sheet. Pressing the tops keeps the top from rounding and no Southern cook worth his pay would serve up rounded-top biscuits.

From scratch:
2 cups flour
3 teaspoons baking powder
½ teaspoon salt
4 tablespoons cold shortening
¾ cup milk
1 to 2 tablespoons melted butter

    Preheat oven to 425. Sift dry ingredients into a bowl. Add shortening and use a pastry knife to cut into flour. Or, using your fingers, work the shortening into the dough until it becomes grainy with pea-sized clumps. Add milk and stir just until the dough comes together. Turn out dough onto an adequately floured board – that is, more than a little but not too much. Pat into a square. Loosen square, fold over, and pat into a square three more times ending with a square 1½ inches thick. Flour dough and tools as needed to keep from sticking, but don't go crazy. Cut out biscuit-sized rounds using an empty soup can or drinking glass, place on parchment-lined baking sheet and bake for 10 to 12 minutes until golden brown. Brush tops with melted butter after done baking.

Sausage gravy
½ pound sausage patty meat
1 cup flour
3 cups milk
Salt and black pepper to taste

Crumble sausage meat into a medium pot over medium heat. As meat begins to cook, sprinkle flour over it and stir. Cook until the sausage is browned. Slowly add milk and stir. At this point I usually switch to a whisk to separate chunks of both meat and flour. Stir occasionally or constantly, as you see fit, adding milk. If you add the milk slowly, you get a better idea of how thick your gravy is. It should be thick, but not so thick it won't spread out when poured over a biscuit. Put the black pepper right to it. Black pepper in quantity has its own kind of spiciness and it adds piquancy to sausage gravy. Salt to taste as needed.

CHAPTER 5
In the Galley

I t's 7:15 p.m. and I'm alone in a four-man room. The room is what only could be called steerage class, two decks as near as I can tell, possibly more, below the galley. I'm lying in the fetal position, left side down with my head towards the foot of the rack. My left arm is behind my back, jacked up in the come-along position as high as I can force it up. My right arm is around the back of my head and my fingers are straining to clasp my chin, hauling my head to face left, while the inflexibility of my arm and shoulder forces my head forward. This tortured position is the most comfortable I can develop and the tragedy of it makes me laugh. My mother, a second grade teacher in public school, once had a poor unfortunate in her class, Donny, who in crisis, like when the bell rang bringing class into session for the day, would reach his right hand around his head to grasp his ear while sucking his left thumb. I feel like Donny.

I am one hurting fifty-five-year-old unit.

After a twelve-hour shift, I am a physical wreck. My hands and fingers are blanched and parboiled from dishwashing and my forearm muscles, overworked and acid-filled, are frozen, drawing my hands into claws. My fingernails are soft and corroded from bleach. My upper back, neck, and shoulders are throbbing knots of white-hot pain, while my hips, knees, and feet are merely red-hot sunspots of ache. The thigh and calf muscles connecting the three joints are thrumming and screaming with overuse. I've had a hot shower and I've taken three aspirin, which haven't kicked in yet. And I have thirteen more days to go in the galley.

The first day is always the worst. The same goes for football camp, basic combat training, the cardiac surgery suite, or Angola State Prison. The physical trials of breaking in as a galley hand are magnified by the fact that Hercules 20 does not have a dishwashing machine, so the flatware and dishes, cups, and glasses have to be washed with a solution of bleach. The hot water is scalding. Good for clean; bad for first-day-on-the-job galley hand. Moreover, the available gloves are for food prep and only come up to the wrist, insufficiently long to keep the water out when you're fishing around for flatware in the bottom of a sink full of dirty dishes.

Physical trials, there are a-plenty. Part of the problem comes from a career as desk jockey. Reporter, editor, writer, and public information officer keep one securely behind the desk instead of behind the plow or the barricade. Even the rigors of cutting, splitting, and stacking wood by hand are long gone since the move to Louisiana eight months ago.

In the galley, everything takes effort. Pans loaded with thawing meat and tucked under the cooking benches require toting from the freezer and bending over. Equally as bad is retrieving them, which requires scooching down and hauling them out, then arising to a stoop and picking it up. Hell, bending over to get the pan from storage under the bench before loading it up elicits an involuntary groan!

And the posture at the sink? ChiCom torture plain and simple. The sink is low. To use it you have to bend over, more than a slump, but not quite a full bow, which would be hellish in its own way. While the spine is supple and capable of bending, approaching old age, the human anatomy supporting the spine gets tired, rusty, and cantankerous. After an hour or so of unusual posture, it begins to bitch and then rebel. Do that for most of the breakfast hour, keeping up with the dishes, and the carcass gets downright revolutionary, engaging in involuntary twitching and spasms that pull the right side of your face into a momentary smile/grimace and shutters your eye. In the next moment, your left arm jerks up and folds it into some kind of chicken wing position with your hand bent maximum at the wrist, poised uselessly over nothing, creating the image of not just old and creepy, but deeply insane too.

Poor aching old tired and stressed muscles, tendons, ligaments, fascia, right on down to individual cells are screaming saying, "For chrissakes, Pat, let's sit down, have a cigar and half-a-bottle of bourbon while we thoughtfully craft our letter of resignation. . . ."

Oh yeah, I want to be a cook on an oil rig in the Gulf, and breaking in in the galley is the way to do it.

The aspirin eventually kicks in and deadens reaction to mere intense discomfort. Sleep follows with crazy dreams and a lot of rolling around trying to get comfortable.

Oddly enough, I'm not the only fossil creeping

around like a bucket of pain. Three of the senior men on this crew are even older than I am. And while they have boss jobs, night tool pusher, motor man, and driller, they're still subject to rigorous daily toil compounded by a lifetime of rig physical abuse, while I have a nicely broken-in bureaucratic padded ass and a high-end eating and drinking pot belly.

"Man, what are you doing out here?" one asks, sympathetically.

"Ahhh, I wanted to have an offshore experience," I respond with a shrug.

Another one looks me over and states, "I think you're one of those guys who retired too early."

I nod enthusiastically in full agreement.

Even more odd, the boss of the whole crew, Dennis, is in his early thirties, maybe half the motorman's age, and is the youngest boss I encountered in a year offshore.

The catering crew consists of Ken, steward, and Carlos, night cook and baker, two bedroom hands, a night galley hand, and me. We're down one utility/bedroom hand.

Ken has led an adventurous life, cooking high and low depending upon his circumstances at the time. He's cooked in fancy New Orleans restaurants as well as metropolitan dives, and he's been offshore as a cook from Florida to Texas.

His grub is always better than just "good," and his etouffee is the best I've ever had. After a couple of days proof, the men are highly complimentary and appreciate his efforts.

There's a certain rhythm to the job of galley hand that only takes two or three shifts to learn. There are an infinite variety of tasks to perform, but the main ones consist of keeping up with washing the plates, flatware, cups, and glasses during the meal, observing the serving line and keeping it inviting, well stocked, and clean, maintaining the salad bar, which is specifically the galley hand's responsibility, and watching the dining room for spills, accidents, or mud boys making a mess. Usually the men are conscientious about spills, and they're careful not to track in dirt, but sometimes things happen. I found it was easier and less work to clean up accidents or tracks myself, rather than have the guys do it, and they appreciated the good will.

The galley hand also is responsible for making coffee, ensuring there is cream and sugar, and filling, maintaining, and keeping clean the milk and soda dispensers. Ice tea, sweet and otherwise, is consumed by the gallon, and the dayside galley hand is usually responsible for that, too.

After meals, the serving line has to be broken down and the dining room needs to be cleaned. Break down is routine, but a pain. The steam table keeps food items hot, but also cooks them even at low temps, so pans of gravies, sauces, and starches need to soak. The cook tells the galley hand what to keep—leftover ham steak will make a nice treat for breakfast and roast chicken can go around again as soup, tetrazzini, or yummy chicken and dumplings. Leftover veggies, juices, and scraps go into the slop bucket for feeding the fishies and the filthy gulls over the side or, if it's a do-gooder rig, into the waste container.

In the dining room, tables and chairs get wiped down and the floor is swept and mopped once per shift. Condiments (mustard, ketchup, mayo, salsas, and hot sauces) are replenished and salt and pepper shakers refilled.

Garbage—which the galley and dining room generate a lot of—gets brought out to the compactor. So too does cardboard, which usually has its own compactor.

Outside on the rig by the compactors, a hard hat, safety glasses, and steel-toe shoes are required. It isn't weird, it just is. Taylors hard hats are orange and have a visor. They're pretty distinctive, and in the Gulf they shout "caterer!" Taylors safety glasses are standard issue, ugly, and resemble the army's mortifying "birth control glasses" of basic training. Cooks and utility hands who have been on rigs for a while or have made pals with rig safety officers usually have cooler and more functional safety glasses resembling the stylish Oakley shades the army sports in Iraq. Occasionally, you'll find a caterer with his own hardhat, decals, scrapes, and scratches, indicating real hardhat work once upon a career. But that's only occasionally.

The galley floor, like the dining room, needs to be swept and mopped once per shift.

Different rigs have different systems their stewards have developed. Making the system work falls to the galley hand. Take fruit juice, for instance. On Herc 20, juices come in thirty-two-ounce cans, twelve cans to a case. Open cans are kept in a refrigerator, and when the men want a drink, they get it using wax paper cups. There are lots of different kinds of juice—orange, pineapple, grapefruit, grape, apple, cranberry, and some mixtures like orange pineapple or cranapple. The cases of juices are kept under a storage shelf at the opposite end of the dining room. There's haphazardness about the storage—it's cramped and difficult to get at and the cases are heavy at more than twenty-five pounds each—so one's inclination on grocery day is to sling the cases in there and be done with it. But doing so shows little foresight, not just because the product isn't being rotated, but also because the guy doing the slinging is going to have to "unsling" them at some point to replenish the fridge. If all the apple or grape is underneath all the cranberry or orange, well, you can see the problem. A little bit of organization could make things better and easier.

Becoming cognizant of situations like that isn't automatic in the first couple of days, but it does occur within the first week. The juice storage situation suggests systemic neglect.

Herc 20 is old and hard-used. A refit might be the most beneficial course of action, but barring that, some professional care in the guise of soap and water and Formula 409 would help. I'm told the rig had a regular steward and crew at one point, but I don't know about now. I'm skeptical, because all of my crew are first timers, with the exception of the night galley hand who has been aboard for fifty-six days and counting. A couple of utility hand replacements come and go—one is "run off" even before his shift is over—and all in all, it seems to be a hard-luck rig.

That view is somewhat confirmed when one crewman asserts the rig has sunk three if not four times in a career spanning more than fifty years. The rig also has a claim to fame, which makes great scuttlebutt, that it was filmed as background for a Sean Connery James Bond picture in the early '60s *Casino Royale* or *Thunderball*, the rumor mill is uncertain which. But of course, it *is* true.

The state of the galley and the rig puts the dayside

crew in somewhat of a quandary. It is filthy. The coolers are dirty inside and out, the floor in the storage room has broken tiles and ground in dirt that needs some serious mopping and bleach, and of course, it also has no dishwasher. The oven and stoves are a grimy mess and the deep fryer needs a change of oil and a thorough cleaning. The dining room demands attention, too.

Below decks, the quarters could use a damn good cleaning, as well. A minimum of sweeping and emptying the overflowing trash receptacles. A maximum of mopping and waxing all floors, washing down walls, changing bed linens and blankets, and hoeing out lockers that have served as dumpsters for creatures, cretins, and simpletons.

The storage room, where the dirty linens and blankets are bagged and awaiting transport to shore, and the laundry is a disgraceful mess, but that could be dealt with in a couple hours of rearranging, some sweat, and a spray bottle of disinfectant

But the nastiest thing, and a mortal sin of apparent long standing, is the gutter at the foot of the cooler in the storage room adjacent to the kitchen. Once lined with aluminum foil and by design built to catch and channel condensation from the cold chest, the gutter now glimmers with vile black liquid and chunks of unidentifiable stuff so offensive and repellant that good old shit in comparison is just smelly human waste.

The foil lining is peeling, ripped in places and folded back in spots so there is no liner, and looking at it, baleful, malevolent, and unmistakable, one wonders what sort of son-of-a-bitch-beast could live, work, and prepare food in its presence.

The question is simple: To clean or not to clean?

The quandary is: I am here temporarily. This is not my rig. I did not create this mess, so why should I be obliged to fix it? If the men who work here regularly do not care sufficiently to maintain minimum standards of professionalism, why should I break hump to make it right for them?

I think it's the universal dilemma of the conscientious, and we wrestle with it for about three minutes. Ken makes an incremental decision: He and the night cook will share the cleaning jobs of stove, fryer, and environs. I will tackle the dining room. The utility hands will start with cleaning the stairs and hallways and the storage room.

No one's happy, and no one likes it. But we have to. Our standards demand it. There's some grousing, but things start to improve. The night galley hand is outraged and, as days pass, he becomes more vociferous. He's not going to do anything. Ken is a usurper and an interloper trying to make folks work hard so that he looks good. And he'll be goddamned if he busts his ass so some temporary steward he'll never see again will earn all the attaboys.

His reaction is so juvenile, so puerile and ignorant, that it is breathtaking. In fact, it won't bear argument and isn't worth deconstructing. So no one argues with him. But for someone whose self importance is going to be eroded by a little extra toil, his position says a lot more about *him* than he thinks, and it also explains why the rig is in the state it is.

The night cook ends up ignoring him altogether, washing his own dishes.

And I end up cleaning the gutter.

A moment's aside here: Paper towels, to my mind, are indispensable. Like Homer Simpson's paean: "Mmmmm donuts! Is there nothing they can't do?" I feel the same way about paper towels. And I have since I helped out in the galley on the Fishing Vessel ShelMac in 1981. Paper towels are slightly expensive and they shouldn't be wasted, but they are there to be used, and they are an essential kitchen tool. They can blot up spills; they can be used to clean things funky and non-funky alike, like toilets; and they can be thrown out without contaminating yourself or others. By themselves or folded, they can give you a temporarily clean surface to set things on or on which to cut. They can be used to dry things, whether dishes or chicken pieces, blood from a cut finger or hand, or a running nose. On a fishing boat once in frenzy faced with a badly damaged drag and considerable labor on the part of the crew to fix it before getting it over the side once more to catch more scallops, the captain and deck officers were shouting, "Time is money!" And so it turned out to be, not just on fishing boats, but virtually everywhere else too in the American business world, whether newspaper, academia, or police station. In a similar vein, paper towels save time.

Herc 20 didn't have any paper towels.

So we used rags and old face cloths and tore old towels apart into face cloth-sized rags and used them as paper towels. Of course they'd get nasty and after half a shift, and I'd have to run them down to the laundry and plead with the utility hand to upset his schedule and throw a load in. It wasn't optimum, but on this plainly forsaken rig, what was?

The plan for cleaning the gutter was carefully devised and executed. In a *High Noon* moment just before I began, I came around the corner from the storage room and no one was in town. The galley and dining room was empty.

Ken had disappeared probably to burn one and suck down an ice cream anywhere but *there*! I armored myself from contamination with medical-grade latex gloves and determined to wildly expend any and all resources to get it done. I took a load of the nastiest towels and a garbage bag and dropped the towels into the gutter to soak up the vile juice. Quite apart from the disgust factor, I truly was cognizant of the relationship between serious disease agents and used cooling water. Legionnaires' disease was connected to air conditioners, and sometimes you can smell the latent disease in cooling tubes of refrigerators and air conditioners. This stuff was concentrated evil substance plus unknown putridity. More than an irrational phobia or a debunked urban legend, there was reason to fear the juice.

Once the rag had blotted up as much putrescence as it could hold, I'd ease the garbage bag adjacent (without getting my face too close to the scene of the crime) so that I could retrieve it with thumb and index finger and lift it up, dripping, and drop it into the bag without the juice touching or spilling onto anything else. Once the gutter was bailed, I used a broom handle to poke and prod the aluminum foil into a jumble, then I carefully fished that out, too, and dropped it into the bag.

Best practices at this point called for the killing power of saintly bleach, so I took a gallon and dumped generous amounts of it into the gutter from one end to the other. Then I took a relatively clean mop and swabbed out the vile alley, not caring if bleach splashed around because the goodness of bleach could chemically overcome and morally overwhelm any residual satanic filth. I rinsed the mop in a steaming hot bath of bleach and detergent and did the whole twenty-foot gutter.

Now it's looking halfway decent. I double bagged the garbage bag with the rags and foil, clapped on my hard-hat and glasses, and ran the bag out to the compactor to get rid of it.

Mr. Ken is still among the missing. The coward.

The gutter was about two-and-a-half inches deep and two-and-a-half inches wide, just about the size of a household aluminum foil box, so I found a similarly-sized box of parchment paper and used the box as a construction mold to build a double layer foil liner. It fit in OK. Although it wasn't perfect, it was a damn sight better than it had been.

And strangely enough, after I dumped the crap water from the mop operation, threw out the mop and replaced the head with a new, clean one, and got everything put away, Mr. Ken strolled in and started on lunch.

Each day the work got a little easier. My improving physical condition was most apparent in the morning, plodding up the stairs to the galley from my room at 5:50 a.m. My legs were sore, but a little less so with each passing day. And I noticed I could bend and retrieve things with neither hurt nor involuntary sound.

I'm getting used to being a bus boy.

From my e-mail to eldest son in Iraq:

I'm baaaaack
March 1, 2007 2:57 p.m.

From: "Patrick Keefe"
To: "Christopher Keefe"

Just got in. I smell like diesel and two weeks confinement. Gads, what an adventure! Did I enjoy it? No. Do I like it? It's too hard to say. The work was unrelenting toil. I really was a scullery maid. I did some salad bar work, some prep, and a little cooking, but mostly mopping, sweeping, and endless dishes and pots and pans, and keeping the dining area clean. Plus lugging five gallon jars of water, emptying garbage bags, and dumping the slop pail over the side. Constant coffee-making too, but the boys liked my dark roast.

The rig was atrocious. Filthy. Both of the cooks, first timers on the Herc 20 but experienced men, said they wouldn't go back, and I was with them when they told the supervisor.

The cook was top notch—he used spices like my old boss Linc Soldati years ago (who was more than a credible cook)—and his etouffee was the best I've had (four times, three different places so far, including Don's, a highly-rated Lafayette Cajun joint).

The men on the rig were great. The experience is priceless, and although I'm glad to be back in Red Stick (This really is a cool place.) for a week, I'm sorta looking forward to the next installment. Honest! But remember, I've had a career, and this is just a lark—even though it's pounding me to crap and I need a chiropractor, a masseuse, a barber, a manicurist, and fifty to sixty beers.

More to come later. Tomorrow, if not tonight. Thanks for your note. I met a couple of
roustabouts (laborers) who were in the Louisiana Guard and were expecting orders to ship
over later this year. Careful Over There. . . .
Love,
Pops-a-rama Galley Hand
(scullery maid)

George Bernard Shaw (an Irishman) is reputed to
have said, "England and America are two countries separated by a common language." Shaw's observation is relevant
to the difference between how Northerners and Southerners
speak and how that difference plays out offshore.

A New Hampshire native, I speak like I'm from
there. It is not an affectation, something I can turn on and
off at will. It's on. All the time. Why wouldn't it be? It's how
I learned to talk. Outside of New England, my accent is considered "Bostonian," and people remark that I sound like
Jack Kennedy. Nothing could be further from the truth. Kennedy spoke pure Massachusetts burnished by a Harvard education. I speak what I consider "Yankee," a lingo my father
used to call "the King's English," and a manner of speaking
found north of Boston, most precisely in New Hampshire
and Maine. Although the Maineiacs have a really broad accent that betrays them for the rubes and hayseeds they are.

Speaking New England is a mixed blessing and has
been all of my life. My college mates in Minnesota were intrigued at the oddities coming out of my mouth. And being
competitive young males, it didn't take too long for them to
mimic saying things like "cah" for automobile and "bee-ah"

for good St. Paul brews like Hamm's or Schmidt's or the male-teen-devastating GBX, Grain Belt malt liquor.

They figured out the dynamic pretty quickly: If a word ends in "R," drop the letter and add A-H, "ah." They also discerned, though this took additional pondering and analysis, that if a word ends in "A," you drop the "A" and add "E-R." Thus "Cuba" becomes "Cuber" and "pizza," "pizzer."

They reckoned the ruckus only breaks out when the letter "R" gets into proximity with the letter "A" or "E," and that is good Yankee.

In northern New England, speaking Yankee is routine; it's how most everyone talks. In mid-New England, Massachusetts, speaking Yankee just marks you as being from points north. In southern New England, Connecticut, speaking Yankee is damnably odd and marks you for the rube and hayseed you are.

In Louisiana, speaking Yankee is indecipherable. Unfortunately, the reverse holds true, too.

"Hawsh freenah frump dishawaba," some Rebel will say.

"I beg yer pahdon." I reply gentlemanly-like.

"HAWSH Freenah Frump Dishawaba," he'll reply with a little more volume, sort of like speaking English loudly to foreigners in their country so that they'll hear *and* understand a language they don't speak.

"Whaaat!?" I assert, appealing to his good nature and seeking help from anyone nearby who can translate the two versions of the same language.

We disengage, walking away shaking our heads. Sure, I missed a chance to buy fifty pounds of fresh shrimp for $20 and I'm glum, thinking, "I have no idea what you just said, my fine-feathered Confederate friend."

Once on Hercules 11, I added some hot-off-the-grill bacon to the breakfast line. The tool pusher, an older gent, came in and I said, pointing to it, "The fresh stuff is in the forward part of the pan."

"Whaaat?" he said.

"The Fresh Stuff is in the Forward Part of the Pan," I repeated, annunciating carefully and indicating where the select goodies were.

The repeat failed. He was silent for a couple of seconds while miscommunication occurred and was analyzed and was determined that it didn't matter and couldn't be that important.

"I have no idea what you just said, son," he muttered.

"There's Fresh Bacon Right Here," I said pointing emphatically and speaking somewhat exasperatedly, even though he was the boss and an older fella.

He ignored me and asked for a ham and cheese omelet.

The difficulty, I thought afterwards, was my fault: not merely Yankee pronunciation, but word selection as well. Since we were in a "nautical" situation, that is, on a rig offshore surrounded by ocean and required to use boats to travel to and fro, I used "forward," a nautical term I learned working on boats as the correct word for "the front section of the boat or something." That was stupid because the only thing nautical about our situation, besides everything, was nothing. We were drilling for oil, an activity that takes place in Texas and sometimes on the ocean. Drillers are oil men, not mariners or seafarers or scallopers.

The miscommunication was compounded by the devilish combination of "a" and "r" in both "forward" and "part" that rendered the phrase in Yankee, "foh-wahd paht."

Hunh? And it was first thing in the morning, he was a native of Mississippi, and, as I said, he was an older gent and probably hard of hearing.

I guess to him it came out as "Hawsh freenah frump dishawaba," and he was saddened thinking, "What's that old fool doing out here, anyways?"

"Hey cookie, gimme a ham and cheese omelet. . . ."

I learned in short order not to answer the phone in the galley. Not just because sometimes it was a soft touch in the control room asking for six lunches to be put up for the boat crew, when at quarter to one most of the grub was eaten or gone, but usually because it was some boss in the control room telling me to do something urgent and I couldn't understand what he was saying.

"Galley," I'd say, grabbing the phone on the second ring.

"Hawsh freenah frump dishawaba," a commanding voice would reply.

"I'm sorry, what?"

"Hawsh Freenah Frump Dishawaba," said a little louder, a little more emphatically, and with considerably more authority. Yet it was all Farsi to me.

"I'm sorry, mister, I got Yankee ears. Let me get someone here who speaks good Southern," I would say, beckoning wildly for anyone to get over here, help out, and get me off the hook.

"He wants us to get Benjy, the mud logger up in

room six, and tell him to report to control pronto," my translator would relay.

"OK. Can do," I say, and set about getting it done while thinking, "How come he didn't say that to me?"

On Herc 20, there was a big redhead roustabout who was relatively friendly going through the line. I was filling in in the change- and laundry-room and he came in.

"How ya doin'?" I asked.

He nodded greeting.

"What's your name?" I asked, thinking it would be good to put a name to a friendly face.

"Tay-um," he said.

"What?"

"Tay-um," he replied a little louder.

"Tay-um?" I asked, wondering what the hell sort of moniker that was.

"Tay-um. Tee Ah Emm. Tay-um!" he said, bordering on losing his temper.

"Oh! Tim! Yes, well that has one syllable in it. . . ." I said, nodding and smiling and moving backwards gracelessly to where I could hide over by the washing machines.

He went about his business and our budding friendship died, a victim of Southern pronunciation and Yankee ears. Would-be brothers separated by a common language.

Hardworking men need to eat well, which is the reason for having caterers offshore. How the caterers pull off the "well" part depends on the cook. In my experience, most of them are solidly good, with a trend towards better than just good, plus an occasional "excellent." Any cook's cooking is improved by seasoning and the proper use of spices, but nothing spells a home-cooked meal like one in which the diner adds his own favorite condiments.

Condiments, by definition, are something used to give a special flavor to food. Offshore, mustard, ketchup, salt, or spices are awesome, expansive, and required. Their importance can be judged by their omnipresence: They most frequently sit in large containers in the middle of the table. The containers are usually custom-made wooden things, made in the shops on the rig, and they often resemble hand-made wooden tool boxes, though not as wide, and they're five or six feet long. Salt and pepper, at the top of the condiment hierarchy, usually sit in shakers on the rim of the containers or are perched on the handle running across the top, along with the toothpick dispenser.

The containers are jam-packed, crammed, and slammed with condiments. Good sized containers, too, industrial, when available, otherwise, large! In no particular order: mustard, ketchup, mayo, squeeze bottles of margarine; strawberry, grape, and apple jelly and preserves; mild, medium, and hot salsas (often two kinds of them: Pace and Tostitos or Old El Paso); Tabasco and Louisiana Hot Sauce always, occasionally Texas Pete, Trappey's or Crystal and frequently Tiger Sauce; squeeze bottles/bears of honey; two kinds of maple flavored syrups and a can of Steen's Cane Syrup; molasses; Cajun Chef pickled hot peppers, slices of jalapeno, and rarely, mild or hot pickled okra; sugar pourers and Tony Chachere's Cajun Seasoning.

Rigs might order something specific for a guy if he's a regular crewman and needs it bad and is a good guy— Cholula hot sauce for example, or raspberry preserves, or muscadine or mayhaw jelly.

The galley hand is responsible for keeping the condiments in the containers and keeping the containers clean. Most of the condiments are liquid, they're sticky, and they drip. The men being men, which is to say slobs by and large, they will always try to wipe up a spill, but dripped honey is just going to tear a napkin and leave shreds behind. Dipping a napkin in a Pepsi to get a little liquid to aid clean up of the honey or Steen's is a conscientious idea, but dumb. It's not going to work because the Pepsi leaves its own sticky footprint.

Taking care of the condiment containers isn't a big deal, but it is something that needs to be done daily. I discovered that it was just as easy as not to remove the container from the tabletop—even though it was heavy—when I cleaned after the morning meal in order to make sure there wasn't mung hiding under the container. The other galley hands were impressed. They expressed admiration, not because it appealed to their sense of cleanliness or professionalism, but because they could rely on the table being thoroughly cleaned once a day. Besides, how much mung can accumulate under a condiment container in twenty-four hours and three meals? A little 409 sprayed around the table and wiped up after breakdown serves as a fine temporary expedient, and the old guy's going to get it tomorrow anyways, so what th' hey.

I didn't mind because I was on a career trajectory to being their boss, and they'd do it my way once I ran the shift.

Galley hands are watched by cooks and stewards, but not that carefully because the cooks and stewards have their own things to do—smokes to smoke and b.s.-ing to do with idle roustabouts and crane operators hiding and gathered around the galley exit smoking and looking to mooch ice cream bars and Mountain Dews.

When a galley hand is not under acute observation, he is empowered, by default, to make decisions. Sometimes he decides to sneak off to meet the bedroom attendant in the laundry, and they'll smoke and talk dirty and drink Mountain Dews. But sometimes he'll use his empowerment to do something not too strenuous, like refilling the condiment containers. Generally that empowerment takes the form of throwing out the container that has three tablespoons of hot salsa left in it and replacing it with a new one.

I approve of this practice. As a caterer in high school, we would consolidate condiments, stacking nearly-empty bottles of ketchup on top of another more full one, and letting the one drain into the other. It cut down on waste and saved money. But that was on a way smaller scale than diddling around with condiments on a rig. I'm aware of starving children in Borneo, although the saved three tablespoons of salsa in no way can benefit them, nor do I approve of waste. Sure the three tablespoons of hot salsa can add up, but to what? Like the inflexible rule that demands your buttered bread falls butter-side down on the floor, almost never when a jar of salsa is low on one table is there one on another table with sufficient room in it to consolidate. Moreover, you can't in good faith mix and match, say adding three tablespoons of hot Tostito's salsa to an available nearly-empty jar of mild Pace salsa. Well, you can, but it seems immoral somehow. If a guy wants mild salsa on his scrambled eggs, fried chicken, or ham steak, then it ought not to be mild/hot Pace/Tostito's salsa. It's just not right, and April 1st only comes once a year. Throw it out and be done with it.

The galley hand is responsible for preparing and maintaining the tomato, lettuce, and onion tray that is required for a burger (or sandwich) to be "dressed" down South. The tray, usually a cafeteria tray covered in foil and bearing sliced tomato and onions and lettuce leaves, isn't difficult to prepare as much as it is difficult to remember. The recollection of it has a direct relationship to the degree of responsibility you bear: If you're responsible for the tray, you'll seldom remember it.

The scenario has two possibilities and only two.

Number one:

"Hey, you got any onions back there?" Jimmy Tom shouts during lunch.

"That damn galley hand," Julius, the steward, responds, looking up and seeing me heading for the cooler to get the tray and put it out.

He chuckles.

'Nuff said.

The other scenario has me in an executive position, but with nearly the same outcome.

"Hey, you got any onions back there?" Jimmy Tom shouts during the midnight meal.

"Yeah, just a second," I say checking the grill to see if the burgers can stand an additional thirty seconds of cooking, which they can because the burgers, like the steaks offshore, are all cooked wellll done. I glance up to see if that damn galley hand is anywhere about, and, of course, he's not. I trot over to the cooler and retrieve the tray to see it was devastated by supper and returned empty, for all purposes, to the cooler after breakdown anyways. There's no tomatoes, two partial pieces of onion resembling paper-thin wedges, and the shreds of lettuce on display are wilted and brown.

"Whattaya want Jimmy Tom, onions?" I ask, hoping for the best but knowing in advance the true answer.

"Yeah, tomatoes, and lettuce too, if ya got 'em."

"Yup. But it'll be a couple of minutes," I say.

"'K," he says. The men are good about things like that. It doesn't have to be immediate as long as it's sometime soon and you don't forget them.

The damn galley hand in the meantime, at that exact moment, has miraculously finished his dishes and taken the precise instant to go down to the laundry to fetch the towels and cleaning rags. He should get back just as I've put out a refurbished tray that will last two, maybe three, meals.

On a production rig, the lettuce and tomato tray comes attached to another heavy responsibility. The men get a sandwich break at 9:00 a.m. and 3:00 p.m. and cold cuts are the sandwich stuffer of choice. There's no fooling around here since the break is ten minutes and that means everyone has to be accommodated in a minimum of time. The tomato tray and the cold cuts trays *have* to be ready.

The day after grocery day is boom time for the cold cuts tray: chicken breast and smoked chicken breast; ham, "Cajun" ham; salami and bologna; plus Swiss and American slices. Even after the chickens and the hams have run out, there is always still enough to top off on; it's just not as "top shelf" as previously.

The men come boiling in at about three seconds past 9, fanning out in an individual free market of sandwich assembly. Some get Dr. Peppers and Cokes; some secure chips or Doritos; others make for the bread; while still others make for the cold cuts tray. If there's not too much crowding about the meats, and alleys and exits get formed to allow easy access and egress, it only takes a couple of seconds to fork up a couple of slices of Cajun ham and chicken and a slice of Swiss, then the sandwich maker vectors off to another ingredient station.

There's no standing on ceremony—efficiency trumps all. If the plates are traffic jammed, never mind, swing by the cold cuts tray anyhow, hook your meat, dump it in your palm, and continue on. If your hand is dirty because you didn't have a chance to wash (and most guys are pretty careful about this, but sometimes ya gotta do what ya just gotta do), merely pause to pick up a couple of napkins or a paper towel and cover your palm with them. They make a perfect temporary landing place for flying cold cuts, cheese, and L, T, and O.

With three pieces of bread, a couple of slices each of Cajun ham and chicken and a slice of Swiss, lettuce, tomato, and onion, mustard, mayo, Tony Chachere's, and jalapeno slices, plus an individual bag of Doritos, a Dr. Pepper, and four Toll House cookies snatched and eaten going out the door back to work, well, there's a snack that ought to hold the hungriest roustabout for the two hours and twenty minutes until he can get back into the galley for lunch!

Somewhere in the deepest recesses of the dining room there lurks a tradition. Strikingly enough, the tradition offshore conforms to the same tradition on fishing boats, and although I can't say for certain, I suspect the tradition holds on steamers and even warships. It is rarely spoken. In fact, I've only heard it spoken of twice in a year offshore.

Occasionally, you'll find evidence that someone participated in one aspect of the tradition, but rarely the other. The tradition could lurk behind the scenes under the counter with the spare boxes of cereal. It could be on top of the soda dispenser or underneath the dessert container. Sometimes it's out in the open, but seemingly ignored by all until after a few days when the supply has to be replenished.

The tradition is crackers, specifically Lance, Captain's Wafers, and saltines, and the other part of the tradition is individual portion cans of Armour Vienna Sausages and potted meat. The fishing boats I was on in Massachusetts in the early '80s offered both crackers and cans of meat. Crackers were consumed with soups and chili, but I never saw anyone eat the meat. Yet it always disappeared.

One time on Herc 11, Julius mentioned in passing he'd be ordering sausages and meat. And once on Todco 205, I saw a ferret-faced fellow who threw something out that appeared to be an empty tin of sausage or meat. It made no noise as it landed in the garbage pail. A couple of minutes later, I was able to go look, and there was a tin in there. But I didn't recognize the guy, and I don't recall seeing him again.

Odd. But perhaps the consumption of Captain's Wafers, potted meat, and Vienna sausages is such a basic comestible requirement that, like baked beans on a scalloper, nothing can get done without them. It's not remarkable the supply diminishes, as fuel does on both oil rig and fishing boat as motors run and the hitch wears on. Like all fuels, you don't see the crackers or tinned meats used explicitly, but you come to expect the output of their consumption and anticipate positive results, whether in harvesting bushels of scallops or drilling for "erl" and natural gas. It takes a foolish fellow to discount the efficacy of crackers and canned meat without ever having considered it!

Crawfish Etouffee

Roux or no roux? Tomato, tomato sauce, or tomato paste? Or no tomato? You can wrangle about crawfish etouffeee with your pals over beers while brewing up a pot, much like you can chili, or gumbo, other bowl foods that seem to have deeply committed partisans. I elect to make a roux because I want the etouffee to be thicker than soup. The one time I made it on the rig without a roux, it was flavorful but thin. In fact, one of the guys stirred it up on the line and said, "Kinda loose, ain't it?" "Yeah, but it's tasty," I replied. He allowed that was possible, but selected something else!

I also use a little bit of tomato paste for color as much as flavor, and I'd be happy to wrangle over it. You bring the beer.

Crawfish tails can be replaced with shrimp, but then your dish is "shrimp" etouffee. Even up North.

3 tablespoons fat (unsalted butter, peanut oil)
4 tablespoons flour
½ green pepper finely diced
¾ white or yellow onion finely diced
1 stalk celery finely diced
1 clove garlic mashed
1 pound crawfish tails
1 ½ cups stock or water
2 tablespoons tomato paste
Tony Chachere's
cayenne
salt
freshly ground pepper
bay leaf
2 green onions thinly sliced
parsley

Heat your pot over medium. Add the fat and then the flour. Stir, and keep an eye on it. When the roux is light brown, "blonde" in Cajun parlance, add the green pepper, onion, celery, and garlic and cook for 5 to 10 minutes. Add the tomato paste, Tony Chachere's, and cayenne to taste, bay leaf and stock, stirring to integrate the parts. Pour in any juices from the crawfish tails. Let simmer gently for 10 minutes. Add crawfish tails, green onion slices, and sprinkle on parsley. Cook for 5 minutes. Serve over warmed-up rig rice and with a baguette. Have your favorite hot sauce on the table.

CHAPTER 6

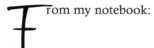

From my notebook:

May 7 11:13 p.m.

So sometime within the last hour or two the realization hit me: I am a cook on an oil rig in the Gulf. The night meal is on—and I'm doing the gravy for breakfast. I'm eating a BBQ beef sammy on a burger roll I toasted and have coffee, water, and Fritos. I'm sitting on a twenty-gallon cardboard barrel—a Chevron recycle slops container—looking at the hermits I made and turned upside down so the bottoms could crisp.

And there was *veritas* in a paragraph. Of course the same elusive *veritas* might also be in a statement or two such as, "You're making $8 an hour!" or "You can't afford to drink Grolsch beer at $14.25 a twelve-pack." But the truth of it was I had achieved my goal; I was a cook on an oil rig in the Gulf.

No bells were ringing, or fireworks shooting off, or chorus of angels sweetly harmonizing in the background as I was lifted aloft for universal praise and admiration. Nothing happened. But it did feel good, even if it was a fleeting sort of thrill. It was an odd goal that required some resoluteness and no little luck, and I had achieved it.

One Monday, post noon, on Herc 11, I found myself leaning up against the sink, eating a bowl of red beans and rice and drinking a Dr. Pepper. Lunch was over and the men were back at work. The steward was off having a smoke, and I was taking a minute to have a bite to eat before breaking down the lunch line.

It occurred to me I was in an extraordinary situation. Here I was, a fifty-five-year-old New Hampshire native on board an oil rig in the Gulf as a galley hand, eating the quintessential Louisiana Monday lunch and drinking the iconic Southern soft drink.

No bells rang in epiphany that time, either. And in addition to chuckling over my situation—odd, damnably odd, Keefe—I think I internalized the moment as a mile marker, or at least a significant something, on the road to somewhere, if not explicitly "goal achievement." Not that eating red beans and rice and drinking Dr. Pepper on a Monday in the Gulf of Mexico was something I set out to do. But it was something I never did in Connecticut in twenty-five years, and it was something I would never have done if I hadn't been in the situation I was. That is, I wasn't just visiting, exposed momentarily to the history and circumstance of New Orleans laundry day, 1790, and lived on 217 years later as a weekly tradition in offshore cookery. I was immersed in it, the culture as regulator of the menu and arbiter of behavior, and I was turning into a freakin' New Orleans Voodoo Queen, fer gawdsakes!

I found myself sweating though, whether from Julius's spicy red beans or my perfervid and idiotic thoughts, I don't know. I do know I scared myself and thought if I didn't cut that crap out right now, I'd soon be reading The Vampire Lestat novel, dropping acid, spending the night in the St. Louis Cemetery # 1, and saying t'ings like "Where yat" for "Where are you [at]?" and "dese" and "dose" and "dem" and "dat."

Good God, man! Pull out of it!

But even pulled out of the fearsome nose dive of sentimentality leading to crash and burn, or worse, "girly-man," or worst of all, "thoughtful," the truth of it is, I did enjoy the situation I was in, preparing and delivering food for the men working offshore. I like making a great meal for the guys, and I like being associated with men who are using their muscles and their brains, plus heavy machinery, technology, and high explosives, to turn a salary and coax a valuable commodity from the earth.

I might like it a little better if I owned a couple of those facilities that produced the valuable commodity from the earth—nothing greedy, just three wells at say between three and five barrels each per day. But hey, who wouldn't?

There are a number of agreeable aspects to cooking. First off is the satisfaction of filling an empty stomach. We live in blessed times with an abundance of food, both fresh and good and manufactured, processed and good, too. The manufactured stuff has a rep as a little less good than the natural, but a corndog on a stick is no moral inferior to a handmade sausage in a gut casing. Now some might posit the corndog is the superior moral product, given that they're both sausages of a sort and therefore filled with lips and gums, hooves and tails, bone chips and ligaments, and ephemera and esoterica of unmentioned parts. But the sausage has a casing made from the intestines of the beastie, while the corndog has an inoffensive manufactured "skin." Sure some might quibble and say the "skin" is a disgusting concoction of leftovers, gelatin, paste, wheat soy, ascorbic acid, and MSG all broken down and smashed and blended together and extruded then dried and formed and sanitized, and they'd be right. But that doesn't make it bad, does it?

Before we get too far along, and for the occasional reader just released from Devil's Island or a Manchurian gulag after having spent the previous half-century incommunicado, let me make this clear. A corndog is a hot dog, spitted on a stick, then dunked in corn batter and deep fried. It's well established as fair or carny food, but street vendors hawk them across the country and they're routinely available now in the frozen junk section of supermarkets. Its antecedents are wrangled over, of course, with the Texas State Fair laying surprisingly plausible late '30s/early '40s originating claims, but the Minnesota State Fair makes an earnest, if less compelling, early-on pitch, too.

Compare then, a corndog to corn on the cob. Both are American foods of repute that are mobile, (relatively) easy to eat, and ubiquitous. That is, they may be found occasionally on a supper table or at the fair or any Louisiana festival. While the piece of corn is a more naturally occurring product, by the time you get done shoving a stick up its marrow and drenching it in butter, salt, black pepper, and

Tony Chachere's, you've altered its back-to-nature goodness and promoted it into something really tasty, but a little less good for you than previously. The corndog, by contrast, isn't at all naturally occurring, but it is natural enough, given the honky tonk of the midway, the crunchiness of its deep fried exoskeleton, the juicy tastiness of its manufactured innards, and its sheer kindliness. Dunk that corndog in mustard—Gulden's or even Kraft, much less Grey Poupon—and your taste buds will all go a-twitter celebrating and excited, and then start asking for beer.

And while corndogs and corn-on-the-cob-on-a-stick are somewhat removed from subsistence foods like potatoes, spaghetti (with or without sauce), peanut butter, Pepperidge Farms bread, cabbage, roots and nuts, vines and trailers, or shoots and grubs, neither is such a lofty climb up the evolutionary food ladder that, from their position, you can't see the bottom, where an empty tummy begins.

What could be more admirable than taking a bunch of raw ingredients and, through skill and imagination and a little chemistry and some judicious heat, turn those basic substances into something yummy. Like cake! Cake is the perfect excuse to cook (namely a yellow cake with a chocolate frosting). For the smart cook, the instructions begin, "Take your box of Duncan Hines® off the shelf and open it."

Even if you're only somewhat clever instead of smart and you have to make your project from scratch, a beautiful yellow cake is only a few ingredients away. While you're pondering the sublimity of culinary creation, I'll be mixing the sugar, flour, butter, eggs, vanilla, a pinch of salt, baking powder, and milk, greasing and flouring the cake tins, preheating the oven to 350, then mixing, pouring the batter into the tins, and slamming them into the oven for thirty-five or forty minutes until done.

See how easy that was?

Frosting is just as easy. While you're contemplating our dessert, I'll be blending softened butter with confectioners' sugar, adding a pinch of salt, fourteen drops or so of vanilla, shaking in some cocoa powder, and adding milk in tiny quantities until I have the right consistency and color. I DO NOT start licking the bowl or implements until the cake is frosted, because one way of running out is to start wolfing down frosting before the cake is fully clothed.

Cake, while approaching the pinnacle of culinary excellence, is, however, not a good antidote to deep down body hunger. For that you need a substance not sweet: meat and potatoes, pasta, chili or gumbo, or a big chunk of fish and rice pilaf.

Meat and potatoes is probably the quickest and the easiest: boiled potatoes take eighteen minutes, and pan frying a steak takes three or so minutes per side from a hot pan. So from start to finish—from nothing to a hale, home-cooked meal—you're talking twenty-five minutes.

In the same amount of time, you couldn't decide on McDonald's; wash your hands; get in the car; go to the ATM; motor to Mickey D's; park; go in; wait in line; order a Big Mac meal; receive it; pour your super-sized Coke; then find a table; sit down; and dig in. Sure the McDonald's satisfies, but your home-cooked meal is better, better for you, and it costs more-or-less the same.

Some folks don't know how to cook; some don't like

to cook; and some folks have never been exposed to cooking. But all like to eat. This, to my mind, poses a problem. In the triumvirate of basic human needs of food, clothing, and shelter, food always come first. Always. You never hear anyone say, "Clothing, shelter, and food," or "Shelter, clothing, and food." It's always, "Food, clothing, and shelter." And that's because the order in which the triumvirate of needs is annunciated, is the order of importance of the needs themselves.

No one responds to being hungry with the statement, "I don't know how to cook," or the only marginally less stupid, "I don't like to cook." What's the matter with you? Cooking is the thing that will respond to the need you're feeling to put something into your mouth. Are you a simpleton? Or just simple? My response is: Let me get my ass in there and make us a couple of burger patties, some eggs, a can of beans, a pot of coffee, and some toast.

A note of differentiation here, not to disrupt a swingin' riff but . . . Americans do not know hunger. And thank God for it. Nothing could be worse. We have a long and deep tradition of being grateful for our many blessings. The abundance of available food is one of those blessings, along with clean water. They're easy to forget, but don't.

Generally speaking, when I'm cooking offshore, I don't eat. Which of course isn't true as baldly stated: I do eat. But not regularly and not very much. There are a number of reasons I don't eat, most having to do with time. Some have to do with what's being served, but that's usually in the context of my health, not the men's.

When I'm cooking, I'm tasting all the time. So I'm ingesting grub, even if it's in increments of teaspoons. I taste virtually everything from cookies to rice to gravy. In the galley, I have paper cups filled with plastic spoons above my work stations so I can taste what's going on. I use taste as the final factor of when something's done or when it needs more seasoning, spices, or heat to be done.

I can't imagine serving something I haven't tasted. How could you do such a thing? The idea to me is not just ludicrous, but unimaginable. Sure, rice cooks in seventeen minutes from the time the water boils again after you've added the rice. But you stop cooking it not when the seventeen minutes are up, but after you've tasted it at seventeen minutes to make sure it's OK and it has the texture you want.

There are certain times during the overnight shift when it's quiet and there's time for a meal. But at 4 a.m., there is no time. You have sixty minutes before the serving line opens. That's when the moving shifts from quick through fast to hypersonic, and you're not going to be taking too much time to sit down and eat. If you sit down at all in the next ninety minutes, it's usually a bad sign. It means something was a disaster that nearly has you beat and contemplating surrender or your wound needs dressing or setting that requires you to be stopped. Other times seem inopportune—when you're breaking down the line from the midnight meal at 1 a.m., the last thing your want to do is start eating. First off, you made the meal and tasted everything two hours ago. Secondly, if you've done it right, there's not too much left but scraps. And 1 a.m. is a weird time to be eating. What is it? Brunch? Late lunch? Midnight snack?

Sometimes a burger feels pretty good during the

midnight meal, especially if the galley hand whipped up a batch of tasty raw materials. I'm doing the cooking, so I can make it how I want, and I usually take half of his portion, reform it, and put it on. I grill the roll, with just a smear of margarine to add some golden brown to it. No cheese. Not cooked too long, but thoroughly, with ketchup for the burger and Doritos if the casing crew—famous for gluttony—didn't eat all the chips. And coffee. A cop's hamburger.

Breakfast would be the meal to chow down on. But two things militate against it. 1) I know better than to turn in ninety minutes later with a stomach-load of bacon, eggs, grits and butter, pancakes, butter and syrup, sausage, biscuits and gravy, coffee and coffee roll, and butter. Ingesting the meal would be a delightful experience, but the aftermath would suicidal acid-stomach-hell. And 2) I don't normally eat bacon, eggs, butter, sausage, biscuits, gravy, or coffee rolls.

Getting off shift on Marianas after a night of running, I'd take two six-ounce cans of juice and a ten-ounce bottle of water. I'd slug them all in my room before showering and make sure I hit the head after the shower to get rid of them before I slept. I needed the liquid, not the grub.

I worked for six stewards. Three as galley hand. Three as night cook/baker. Night cook is a little weird because it can be a fill-in position. Like Herc 21, when the regular steward got his time off, the regular night cook rotated to steward, and I came in for two weeks to fill in. Ideally, a rig will have a regular set of caterers on schedule and rotating as prescribed. The ideal doesn't work too well because of chance, mischance, and instability inherent. That is, the instability inherent in the guys hired for the catering crew. Remember, catering is a competitive undertaking featuring a lot of work, long hours, and low pay. Given the people who populate that station, instability is rather a virtue, since it indicates a willingness to quit to try something (Anything!) else in an effort to better yourself or improve your circumstances. That doesn't mean the choices you make will guarantee success. For some, the choices they make could mean a return to Angola, this time maybe forever. But regardless of outcome, it was a choice freely, if perhaps badly, made.

Caterers get tired or sick. Caterers can wander off or go to jail. They can get shot and need to recover or get shot and fail to recover. They can take up cab driving or work at the casino or run a few numbers. They can sell some cars they never knew were "stolen," or trade commodities, such as a dime bag of reefer or a hit of crystal, for cash or engage in a host of other occupations including "unemployed."

I never managed to get down a regular rotation. The closest I came was two trips on Hercules 21 and the third looming two weeks off. But being the naïve waif I was, I lit out for Maine for those two weeks and didn't inform the company I was going out of state. If I'm off, I'm off, I reasoned, quite incorrectly as it turned out. When the steward recovering from surgery was too quick off the recovery bed and too quick to return to work and unable to complete his shift after four days back, they needed to replace him. They called me at home with the number they had, and I wasn't available. So they hired a new cook who took up my rotation. The new cook was my former galley hand, who, after high school and a lot of horsing around, promised his mother to get a job and keep it.

He had previously worked for one of the huge pizza chain restaurants and attended their "Pizza University." He also expressed interest in becoming a cook, but mostly he was interested in becoming a steward. One Sunday night, I let him make the meal and he came up with pizza, Italian ham, and potatoes. The ham was a large shoulder he marinated in Italian dressing and put in a low oven. Then he made the pizza from scratch according to Pizza U specs. It was a pretty big production, as these things usually are when someone new is cooking and hasn't mastered the idea of minimizing the mess, because you've just got to clean it up afterwards. I offered galley support and help. I shredded the tons of cheese he wanted and made sure oven temps were right (trickier than it ought to be, but adjusting things to four hundred when the numbers on the knobs are worn off is a hit or miss proposition). I kept the workplace uncluttered and the tools and pots and pans clean and back in their place for ready access. I did not offer decision-making or advice, and I pointedly refused to carve the ham, thinking the experience would do him good.

Everything turned out OK, and the pizza was mighty good. The men ate four-and-a-half sheet pans of it.

Ironically, before I left for Maine, I wrote a recommendation to Taylors for him. It was a good report, accurately reflecting his abilities and potential. Returning to Louisiana at the end of my two weeks off, I checked in to get my departure date to find I no longer was scheduled on the Herc 21 rotation. I reckoned the recommendation helped because he got my job!

My next assignment came soon enough, a couple

of days later, to Lake Barre, a production rig, where I was steward, galley hand, and utility hand. It was a temporary assignment from the outset—ten men for a week. That was fine because I was looking for a posting and the idea of a new site was appealing.

The assignment itself was half arsed. Initially, it was supposed to be a two-week assignment. Then there was some question over what, exactly, the assignment was. I was told to contact the company to determine what they wanted. The departure point was a place I'd never heard of and uncertainties ensued.

"Muzhiwuzhiah," the dispatcher said.

"Whaaat!?"

"Muzhiwuzhiah."

"Spell it for me, will ya? I wanna make sure I get it right."

"C-o-c-o-d-r-i-e."

"Cocodrie. Where is it?"

The dispatcher responded, but said something noncommittal like, "It's on the coast. It's in Muzhiwuzhiah parish. Look on the map. I dunno."

I contacted the company via the number provided and was told the position was as cook aboard a production platform for ten men for a week or less. The departure point was indeed Cocodrie, and I was supposed to be there at 5:00 a.m. tomorrow, Saturday.

If you look at a map of Louisiana and find Houma, then look south, you'll see Terrebonne Parish. There doesn't seem to be too much there, but if you've lived through winter in Canada and then been kicked out of New Brunswick, Nova Scotia, or Prince Edward Island, themselves no holiday resorts, and half your family has been murdered, then perhaps the swampland would be Terrebonne, "Good Earth" or "Good Land" or poetically, "Land of Plenty." Because there's plenty there: fish and birds in the billions; gators, prehistoric half-dinosaur and half-crocodile relics called gar; animals; reptiles, amphibians, and rodents of unspeakable size; spiders and insects; brackish water and forty-eight gazillion, quettahillion mosquitoes. In the summer, it's so humid you can *see* the air.

A swamp may not be the best place to raise a family, but if you can get used to it, it's not too bad and beats having the wife and kiddies shot, scalped, and their bodies thrown into the inferno that was your farmhouse. In fact, if you can get used to it, after ten generations, people will think you're cute, and they'll make special license plates and aprons celebrating "Cajun Power." or "Unofficial Coonass," and be charmed when you grunt and point saying, "We go dere, you, unh?"

The map will also show three roads leading south and east out of Houma like arthritic claws. Route 24 heads southwest before ending in Larose, twenty-five miles away and through which the caterer departing from Port Fourchon, with its own particular end-of-the-world desolateness, has to pass.

Of the four roads heading directly south from Houma or branching off Route 24, two stop in the middle of the swamp after passing through villages, and two combine to stop in Cocodrie. That's it for the highways and byways of Terrebonne Parish. It's 135 miles from Baton Rouge to Cocodrie and no direct way to get there. MapQuest reports it takes two hours and forty-one minutes to drive the route, but working things backwards, that means a 2:00 a.m. departure to make a 5:00 a.m. embarkation. However, I've been to Louisiana end-of-the-world spots, like Venice and Fourchon, in the dark hours, and despite being a competent navigator, I always get in trouble. It's the night and the bad signage, and the lack of light, and the poor eyesight, makes navigating from A to B-in-the-middle-of-nowhere such an adventure.

So building in a couple of hours for wandering about stupidly means a midnight departure.

The navigating was tricky, and a couple of times I was turning around and crossing narrow bridges over bayous. Around 3:00 a.m. I was in the vicinity of my destination and could see the orange glare of flame in the sky. In Kenner or Baton Rouge, Shreveport or Morgan City, the orange glow of flame in the sky doesn't bother me. It's a petroleum-based flaring off process and it's a pretty, capitalist sight. But deep in the Southern countryside on a Saturday morning at 3:00 a.m., my Irish superstition, innate cynicism, and Yankee trepidation exerts itself fully and I'm suspicious the glow can only be from a ritualistic gathering, probably surrounding a burning cross. Even worse, the glow waxes and wanes—not regularly, but irregularly and in huge degrees. One moment it's just an orange glow illuminating the landscape, and the next moment it's an orange glow reflecting the ignition of at least twenty additional crosses.

Being thoroughly modern, I find I am unarmed in terms of firearms *and* faith. And since this is Lou'siana, I heartily resolve to do something about the former and hie me unto the gun shop at the earliest opportunity! I'm certainly foolish, too, and historically inaccurate, because this is the very heart of Cajun country. And Cajuns aren't in the Klan or of the Klan and wouldn't abide the Klan. Cajuns— Catholics and swamp-dwellin' critters—were one of the groups the Klan loathed.

Approaching an intersection, I bear right which, ascending slightly, soon resolves the mystery of the orange glare. It is indeed a flare off, but the waxing and waning results periodically from a monstrous jet of flame consuming a huge burst of inflammable something. The event isn't soundless either. The issue of the gas is accompanied by a whizzzzzhhhhhh-eacchhhhk instantly followed by a VVOOOORRRZHEAGH of combustion. It's loud and appalling. I've always been of the mind that true spectacle is elegant and understated. This flare off is neither. It is loud, brash, ignorant, and flashy, like Las Vegas, complacent in its showmanship and power to impress, and therefore less than awe-inspiring. However, it's still pretty damn scary.

By bearing right, the road wends slightly upwards. This is a country road if ever there was, and although technically it has two lanes, it's really a lane-and-a-half, with no shoulder on either side and scarcely any place to turn around. Meet a semi or a fire truck on this piece of property and someone's going to be in the pukka brush. I drive on for a few minutes and notice, there, ahead, is another glow. This is a minor cousin of the monster serving as the beacon of hell below, a mere bonfire of middling proportions. As I approach, I see a scattering of pick-ups and cars and a few people milling about around the fire. There's a body of water close to where the bonfire is, and the attendees don't look either drunk or crazed, but what does one do in Cajun country at 3:30 a.m. on a Saturday morning in June? My experience with the situation is limited, but normally if I'm out around the bonfire at 3:30 a.m., it's a residual of having been out since previously—from the night before—and I'm likely both drunk *and* crazed. Rarely, if ever, have I gotten *up* to be at the bonfire at 3:30 a.m. Other questions include: "What are you doing?" "Why does it take so many of you?" "Mind if I join you?" "Got a beer?"

The road ends at an intersection with a sign showing Route 57—I've made a wrong turn and I've just driven west, maybe five or six miles, across country and away from my destination. I turn around and head back, pass my pals at the bonfire, and exit right onto Route 56 heading for Cocodrie proper, which isn't too much of anything when I get there. It's dark, only periodically illuminated by the eruption of flare off Vesuvius. There are the usual cranes and construction equipment and piles of pipe and casing, plus trailers perched on stilts above surge-tide high-water mark serving as headquarters, offices, dispatch points, and bunkhouses for the fortunate. There's a parking lot with one or two other vehicles coming or going and a bayou where a few boats are docked. We'll be leaving at 5:00 or 5:30 a.m., dispatch tells me, so come back in sixty or ninety minutes and away you go.

I return to the car and figure I'll catch up on an hour's kip, so I grab my Mexican blanket and my Taylors three-panel foam rubber life preserver, which makes an excellent pillow, soft and flexible, and settle in. The car doors have been open for a couple of minutes and when I close them, the interior is a-buzz with mosquitoes. Vicious little bastards, too. Fast, and in vast numbers—twenty or thirty maybe—and apparently hungry as hell for white boy blood.

Cooking

An Asian—Confucius or Buddha or Kwai Chang Caine—was lecturing an American on TV or in a newsmagazine about westerners' fascination with size and power, using the lion and the elephant as examples. True, they are powerful and magnificent animals, he conceded, but what precluded westerners from considering and being awestruck by the ant, able to tote seventy times his own weight, or the mosquito, a rickety assemblage of filaments and air, yet capable of evoking annoyance, full-scale futility, if not despair?

There's acuity in the idea, if not wisdom, or else the learned wouldn't have made the point, I guess. And I can surely testify to the annoyance, futility, and despair. There's no sleeping with a carload of mosquitoes. You're vulnerable everywhere, and hence jumpy, suspicious, and paranoid. Even if you cover up, you're still at risk for actual blood sucking and, worse, psychological exploitation. Curled up in the passenger's side corner with your head resting against your Taylors life preserver and your Mexican blanket providing warmth and supposed mosquito insulation, there are still so many exposed parts of you that it's a joke. Mosquitoes, trapped inside the car with you, hover and whine, dodge and flit, barrel roll, Immelmann turn and crash dive, pull out tiny steels and gleefully strop their proboscis. Then they think about where they're going to nail you and you alert to these PSYOP vibes and slap yourself on the ear. At which point they nail you hard on the right ring finger or just below the ankle bone.

I did not manage to sleep. In fact, I adopted a strategy, although not the finality of the Alaskan caribou, which is to cast himself into the Chukchi sea and drown from attempting to escape assault of the mosquitoes; I merely evac-

131

uated to the out-of-doors, where I hung around listlessly, watching daylight break and other would-be passengers collect. Oddly, the skeeters outside were nowhere near as savage as those inside.

Transportation out of Cocodrie was on a smaller scale than what I was used to. I've gone out to rigs on crew boats 100 or 120 feet long with triple diesels capable of speeds twenty to twenty-three knots (twenty-three to twenty-six mph). The Lake Barre crewboat was thirty to thirty-five feet with twin diesels. It could scoot right along, twenty-six knots (thirty mph), and the skipper was pretty handy, moving the craft from one berth to another with no tiller, just using the throttles.

The boat dropped off day workers at a couple of sites, then it took me to the production platform.

I was transported back to the lumber camps of 1930. The platform—the Lake Barre Commingling Facility—was a collection of wooden structures of varying heights and sizes on wooden pilings. The main building was a white-painted one-story building with windows that had been shouting for fifty years, "Camp Boss rules here!" The neighborhood of the platform was littered with the remains of oil exploration. Wooden pilings sprouted here and there, outlining the existence of once-productive wells and platforms. Derelicts and abandoned sites dotted the seascape, too, and a couple of structures were occupied with crews dismantling them. Petroleum under Lake Barre gave a lot of men a living over the course of the years, and it's still giving.

The facility's crew was splendid. The boss was "Koko" Boudreaux, a Cajun from Dulac, up the road apiece from Cocodrie, and a man who had experienced existence from the subsistence side. He could run the commingling facility and a crew, but at one point early in his life he could hunt, fish and trap, skin and sew, cook, build, barter, and swap so he and his family could live.

Koko grew to enjoy my cooking, suggesting I should quit catering and "go off to be a chef in a fancy restaurant somewheres like New Orleans" and granting me honorary Coonass status for my biscuits, crab cakes, and rémoulade, or "dip" as he called it, cornbread, grilled fish, desserts, and more. In view of my accent, he gave me the designation "Yankee Coonass." I was deeply moved, coming as it did from an original Coonass.

The ten men I was supposed to cook for almost immediately decreased to six, then four. Wednesday, they got a call from HQ telling me to pack up. I'd be on the Thursday morning boat. They called back a little later, realizing they could save $150 by putting me on the 5:00 p.m. Wednesday boat, and so it came to be. It's probably just as well I left when I did. The guys ate well and seemed to be visibly expanding around the middle.

I was back in Baton Rouge at 8:30 that night, only a little displaced at returning to the 21st century from an early 20th century lumber camp on Lake Barre.

Lasagne (and marinara)

Lasagne has been a Keefe family staple since the mid-1960s, when my mother cut a recipe for it out of the Boston Globe. The recipe was by Mrs. Bellotti, Massachusetts Lieutenant Governor Francis X. Bellotti's wife. I think my mother perceived there wasn't anything too objectionable in it for meat and potatoes kids (and husband) and took the dare. It was a brilliant decision. Its place in the Keefe culinary firmament was fixed by Boss Soldati, whose lasagne surpassed even Mrs. Bellotti's recipe by Mrs. Keefe.
My lasagne's decent.

Marinara
28-ounce can of whole peeled tomatoes
1 medium white or yellow onion, small dice
2 cloves garlic smashed
3 to 4 tablespoons olive oil
1 teaspoon dried basil
1 teaspoon oregano
1 teaspoon parsley
1 bay leaf
Tony Chachere's
½ teaspoon red pepper crushed or cayenne. (I like more.)
Tomato paste (if needed)
2 teaspoons sugar (if needed)
Salt and pepper to taste

Place pot over medium heat and add olive oil. Sauté onions and garlic. Stir occasionally. Dump tomatoes into a bowl and crush with your hands. Squeeze the tomatoes between your fingers until they're broken up, and add tomatoes and juice to pot. Sprinkle on herbs and Tony Chachere's, stir, and bring to a boil. Turn heat down to simmer once a boil is reached. While sauce cooks, taste it for flavor and look at texture. Remember, it's a sauce, not a stew. If it needs thickening, add tomato paste. But be judicious. If the paste acidifies the sauce, cut it with the sugar. Let simmer gently and reduce heat. Taste and adjust seasoning. The sauce doesn't take all day. It can cook in twenty minutes and shouldn't take more than an hour. Additional cooking makes the place smell good, especially in winter, but may not help the sauce and, in fact, may hurt it. Determine doneness with a "dynamite" and settle with yourself on taste. (Chapter 2).

Lasagne

Lasagna or lasagne? Lasagna "a" is a single noodle, although it's how the dish has become known in the U.S. Lasagne "e" describes a number of lasagna noodles and is how the dish is known in Italy and elsewhere. I use "e" because I'm using more than one noodle. It's not snooty, it's just numbers.

Making lasagne may look like a lot of work, but it's not. Remember, difficult-to-make dishes don't get made offshore because there isn't time. Moreover, once you've made it, the cooking time gets quicker and quicker. The end result is worth it, for sure!

There are five distinct steps. Make sauce. Boil noodles. Cook meat. Whip up ricotta. Assemble. You can do all four at the same time, whipping up the ricotta while the sauce simmers, the meat cooks, and the noodles boil.

Purists and Italian daughters of all ages might quibble about making the sauce and meat separately. That's rig convenience. Offshore, I make a big batch of sauce and use it for a number of dishes, several of which don't call for meat, which is why I keep them separate. Otherwise, by all means, make a beautiful tomato-meat sauce. Your lasagne will be that much better!

4 cups marinara sauce
1 pound lasagne noodles
2 tablespoons salt
1 pound Italian sausage
2 tablespoons olive oil
1 12-ounce container ricotta cheese
1 egg
½ teaspoon nutmeg
1 cup shredded mozzarella cheese

Preheat oven to 375. Fill a large pot with two gallons of water, bring to a boil, add two tablespoons salt, and boil noodles for five to eight minutes. You don't want them to cook, but you do want them to soften. Drain, then run some cold water over them to keep them loose and stop the cooking. Set aside.

Place a fry pan over medium heat and add two tablespoons olive oil. Cut open Italian sausage and crumble meat into fry pan. Throw out the casing. Stir to brown meat. When browned, add marinara sauce to meat. Bring to temperature and shut off burner.

Dump ricotta into a bowl. Crack in an egg, add the ½ teaspoon nutmeg and half the shredded mozzarella. Stir to mix.

Assembly

In a 9-inch square by 2-inch baking dish, ladle some sauce into the bottom. Layer noodles, sauce, noodles, cheese, until ingredients are used up. For top layer, ladle on sauce, then sprinkle on remaining mozzarella. Cook for 45 minutes until blazing hot. Let set for 10 minutes before cutting.

CHAPTER 7

Marianas

An idle night cook/baker is a terrible thing to waste, and Taylors didn't do it. I was eager for another assignment, especially since Lake Barre, originally designed as short, had been cut even shorter. The dispatcher said there were a number of opportunities, but first, it would be beneficial to get certified with BP safety training. You know BP, British Petroleum. Considering it is a damn oil company whose very existence depends on forcibly extracting natural resources from an earnestly-resisting Earth, in all kinds of climates in all kinds of environments all around the globe, the company is shamefully coy about its business. It loudly proclaims its eco-friendliness in commercials on television. In training sessions, company officials preach that its positions and sensitivities result in about $100 million a year in costs. Adhering to self-imposed policies may give it cachet with environmental crazies—until something goes wrong, then the crazies'll be on the company like fire ants on a co-ed at a picnic in Florida. Call me cynical, but I don't think the posing is worth $100 million. Although, what do I know?

BP training consists of four hours of dos and a lot

of don'ts. Do fight the fire. Do pay attention to safety signs and procedures. Do wear your seatbelt at all times, even in the parking lot, because if you don't and you're seen, then you're gone.

Most importantly, offshore, do not throw anything over the side. No butts. No matches. No garbage. No nothing. If you get caught tossing something overboard, you're gone. With that in mind, I made it a point to spit overboard, and I would have peed overboard, too, and worse, if I could have.

Anyhow, with the training over and successfully completed, I get an offer I could sorta refuse. There's a night cook position open on Marianas, but the night cook position isn't open for a week and they need a utility hand right now for a week. So the deal is: Take the utility hand position—a self-demotion—for a week, then cook for a full fourteen-day shift.

It's an intriguing offer. Marianas is the best Taylors assignment. It's mythical and legendary—even the most humble Taylors scullery maid on the meanest barge mud-bucking off Placquemines Parish somewhere has heard of the mighty Marianas. What are the inducements? Well, cable in every room. Wireless access. Weight room and sauna. After that, it gets pedestrian pretty quickly: decent chow, a full complement of hands, comfortable beds. There doesn't appear to be a third tier of inducements, the first two suffice until you examine them.

Cable TV in every room? That's not a boon to me. I hate TV. It interferes with my sleep, and I shut it off, much to the consternation of the other hands.

Wireless access? That could be useful. OK. A boon.

Weight room and sauna? The sauna could be OK. No. The sauna could be spectacular. Yup, for sure. A boon.

Weight room? No boon. I've been on rigs with a weight room or impromptu gym and never used them. Too tired. I did use the open-air gym on the Apache platform, but that was because I was off at 6:30 or 7:00 p.m. and had a little time before sundown and nighty-night. Marianas did not offer platform-type hours.

The other inducements are meaningless. Decent chow? Of course it's going to be decent. I'm making it! Comfortable racks? I'm going to be comfortable wherever I go because I'm too old and I won't tolerate it otherwise. On Herc 11, I inherited a broken down old rack. I built it up with towels, extra blankets and life preservers and slept soundly, evenly, and with adequate back support for the rest of the trip. Full complement of hands? The crew always seemed to get topped off eventually everywhere anyhow. So despite some occasional dislocation, that's pretty standard fare.

It didn't take too long to decide. I wanted to try it. I was a sufficiently good galley hand, so from that vantage point, I figured, I could scope out the kitchen and have the lay of the land well in hand before I was responsible for my shift.

With BP safety/eco-propagandizing in the afternoon and shift change the next morning in Houma, the company was obliged to bump for a hotel. I scratched around for a high-end restaurant, and I had a notable Italian meal. I returned to the motel and turned in early because a 4:30 a.m. move-out time to get to the airfield at 5:00 a.m. *is* early.

Marianas was sufficiently far off, so that the trip out was by helicopter. We were packed in, as it was crew change day, and even then, I was slated for the second trip. "Good thing I got here at 4:50 a.m. to make an 8:45 a.m. flight," I thought.

I get my first glimpse of the fabled Marianas through the chopper's front windshield. From the angle we're at, it looks like a ship, but it's actually a semisubmersible. That means part of the rig can be flooded to drop below the surface and thus improve stability. "Sink" also works to describe the action, but looses demons of its own that are better left unexamined.

The rig is gigantic, and the huge derrick is enclosed in a house-like structure at the base and some sheathing two-thirds of the way to the top. I haven't seen anything like that before, but none of the rigs I've been on or seen have been this size. I don't especially favor the view, but I didn't know at the time it'd be the last I see of anything for three weeks!

We troop inside and the caterers collect in the office of the camp boss. I make a pitch to be the galley hand, but after a moment's non-consideration, that's rejected. I'm the new guy after all, and the nightside galley hand is regular crew and a Taylors employee of long standing. I'm detailed to the laundry. OK. To the laundry it is, then.

I get my room assignment, 317A, which is my birth date, and the letter designates my bunk and my laundry bag. I make my rack, turn in, and sleep well, making up for the 4:30 a.m. wake-up call.

The best thing that can be said about the laundry is: It's tricky and hard work. Maria from Houston, a Taylors employee and a regular crew member on Marianas, shows me around and comes back a couple of times to help with things I can't figure out. Bless 'er! The laundry is respon-

140

sible for the bedding and the men's dirty clothing coming off shift. You have twelve hours to wash, dry, fold, and return their clothes. There are upwards of 150 workers on the rig—women, as well as men. Of the dozen or so women, half fill administrative roles for BP, like safety officer, medic (nurse), or dispatcher, and the other half are on the catering crew, in the laundry, and in the galley. Figuring half of the 150 on one shift and half on the other, that means the potential of seventy-five loads per shift just for clothing. Towels and face cloths come in from the shower rooms by the score each shift, and with contractors and consultants coming and going there's constant bedding to be done.

On Thursday, shift change, there is bedding change and that causes a spike in the number of loads, often in excess of 100.

There are five washing machines, big, commercial triple- or quadruple-loaders, but only four of them work. There are also five commercial dryers, but one of them only runs on full blast—and as I learn, it's a good idea to temper down the temperature as the load dries because an armful of dungaree overalls just out of a commercial dryer is an amazingly hot product, not merely uncomfortable, but downright painful. Plus the random blistering power of hot brass buttons, zippers, and stainless steel fasteners has to be experienced to be believed. But not more than once.

Keeping track of the laundry is tricky, too. Cause for high anxiety for a new guy; considerably less for an experienced laundress. Crewmen getting someone else's laundry tend to react in the range from annoyed to hostile. Part of the reason is routine. Usually they're counting on getting up, retrieving their clean clothes from the laundry bag hanging on their door handle, donning them and heading off to chow and then work. They usually have it figured so that no time is wasted and they've allotted just enough seconds to do what needs to be done and no more. Anything that upsets the routine understandably upsets them, and receiving someone else's work clothes counts as an upset. It's not just the inconvenience of having to track down your own duds, however that's going to work. Higher values could be at stake. Suppose it was your "oil-finding" overalls? Your lucky socks? Your "safety" T-shirt from Moby Dick's in Minneapolis? Nosiree! Screwing up laundry is not a good practice for a hospitality employee.

While not quite a smooth running machine, the laundry manages to be fairly reliable in getting clothes from Point A to Point B. Bedroom hands bring in the laundry and throw the men's bags into a pile at the entrance. They toss the towels and facecloths into a fifty-gallon plastic garbage pail, and the sheets, pillowcases, and blankets into a couple of other industrial-sized garbage pails. The laundress then uses executive authority to decide what to wash first. Clothes have priority, but there is a steady demand for fresh linen and towels too, so she needs to strike a careful balance. And constant motion is required because the laundress is also responsible for maintaining the adjacent change room and restrooms, as well as for making up the racks in the rooms off the hallway adjacent to the laundry. Some of those rooms have priority because, in addition to housing many of the transients aboard, a couple of the rooms house Taylors staff, including the camp boss.

When a laundry bag is grabbed, the number is recorded on a yellow legal pad. The bag is then dumped out and the contents enumerated. Each item of clothing has to be marked with the bag's number and counted and entered on the yellow pad. The number of pieces is entered on the pad, too, so that when finished, 316A with five pieces *has* five pieces. Check. Tedium ensues, but peril also. Clothing is marked with a Sharpie. It's good for marking, but not so good for writing legibly on cloth or duds soaked from sweat. Poor penmanship poses an experiential threat, too, because imprecision in making a "4" could make it look like a "9." Suppose in a combined load—the only way to do ninety-five plus loads in a twelve-hour shift—you're washing 304A, 304B, 309A, 309B, and 309D. Ill-formed numbers or letters can result in confusion or misidentification, 309A getting 304A's skivvies, and the ensuing rollicking bad time.

Maria and Birdie, who replaced me in the laundry when I went over to cooking, avoided this unpleasantness by being, and writing, like chicks. Maria suggested, and I took all of Maria's suggestions to heart, that assiduity in the laundry would yield gratifying eventualities, although she didn't use those words. She was right, too. With each passing day, my productivity increased and I did successfully do eighty-eight loads in a shift, keep my bedrooms clean and made up, and hit the changing room and restrooms for clean, wipe, mop, and swipe, but I was never able to surpass the ninety-load mark or keep the laundry as squared away as the ladies who dwelt there.

There's a learning curve in undertaking a new assignment. Even for an experienced and self-confident cook, a new assignment means new things: a different galley, unfamiliar equipment, and working conditions that have to be experienced before they can be incorporated into the work pattern. None of these are obstructions as much as they are minor hindrances in transitioning from a new situation to one that's familiar. Once they have been encountered, you begin the process of accommodating them in order to obtain mastery of the situation.

Transforming to night cook on Marianas required the same learning curve as all my other assignments. One advantage was the separation of night cook and baker duties. One hundred fifty men is a large complement that can eat a lot of both supper *and* dessert. So the usual combination of night cook/baker was split, with more than enough work for each to validate the separation. I didn't have to worry about cakes, cookies, and pies, just filling the ten holes on the line.

Another advantage of the circumstance was James, the baker, who was ordinarily the night cook. James seemed happy to be relieved as night cook and take over baking. As baker, you still have plenty of work to do, but the pace is more moderate, the responsibilities less heavy, the routine less frenetic. But James also knew where things were and how they worked, and he was happy to have a new guy do his old job. He also believed in fledglings taking wing on their own, so he wasn't overt in offering aid breaking in a new guy. In fact, he was downright reluctant. However, he was always gracious and very willing to help when asked.

The disadvantage was cooking for nearly three-times as many as I normally cooked for on Herc 21.

The differences were exaggerated, too, by the need for so much variety. Quantity can be adjusted without too much difficulty. If you're making a steak, making three more at the same time isn't too much trouble. But if you're making a steak, and you have to make fish and chicken potpie, too, then that's different. After a couple of shifts, I needed professional counseling and sat with the camp boss to settle on a menu. He gave me a sheet all prepared and approved with columns of days of the week and fifteen slots underneath each day. The fifteen slots represented all the items necessary to fill the ten holes on the line: soup, healthy choice, main meat, rice, beans, vegetable, vegetable, alternate meat, starch, gravy, vegetable, vegetable, meat dish, French fries, breakfast.

The chart was regular and periodic where it could be. The healthy choice was alternately boneless, skinless baked chicken breast, or baked fish. The rice selection was white, wild, or yellow, with brown thrown in once a week to make things episodic rather than routine. The gravies consisted of white, cheese, and brown, with cheese on Saturday and Tuesday, as necessary components of Steak Day, and white was always on Sunday, Fried Chicken Day. Besides, there's only so much you can do with gravy.

The French fries rotated between plain, "home fries," and "potato logs." "Home fries" mean the commercial frozen squares of grated potato that go from freezer to deep fryer and are repellent and delicious at the same time. "Potato logs" are the equally as deadly "tater tots," just crying out for ketchup and a Bayer aspirin to moderate the heart attack until you can get to the doc's and the cardiac catheter lab. Neither home fries nor tater tots *have* to be deadly. They can be baked, but why when you're pressed for time and they're intended to fill number nine of a ten-hole cafeteria line? *Attenzione*: You're not remembering that "the deep fryer is my friend." Moreover, the men could care less, so make it easy and drop 'em in the oil.

Sometimes offshore terminology lacks precision. For instance, on Friday, "Seafood Day," the main meat was shrimp. The "alternate meat" that day was catfish and the "meat dish" was seafood gumbo, suggesting the corollary: Fish, the other meat.

Thoughtful readers will also have noted the concepts of "alternate meat" and "meat dish." Officials might be reluctant to go on the record in differentiating between the two, but the categories nominally exist so the finicky have a chance of getting something they might like. Most importantly, the categories help to fill the endless holes in the grub line on Marianas.

Say some old redneck hates ham. Of course, it's not likely; in fact, it's almost impossible if the guy is a real redneck. But it's just an example so we'll pretend. Ham is the main meat offering on Wednesday. The alternate meat that day is "steak fingers," strips of beef that are treated like chicken nuggets, that is, breaded or coated and deep fried. The steak fingers could be "real," commercially prepared breaded beef of an indeterminate cut that's just dropped into the fryer. But they could be "imagined," generic beef that the cook turns into steak fingers with knife-work, egg wash, and flour or breading mixture. And into the oil it goes.

Alternate meat offerings during the week bear in mind offshore menu custom—Steak Day (Saturday and Tuesday), Seafood Day (Friday), and Fried Chicken Day (Sunday). They are turkey patties, meat loaf, "green peps" (sausage and peppers), steak fingers, chicken strips, catfish, and hot dogs. The meat dish offerings that week are meat loaf, beef potpie, beef patties, meat pie, turkey patties, jambalaya, and chicken potpie. Thus, on Wednesday, our ham-hater can select steak fingers or meat pie—a Cajun specialty that resembles a pasty or an empanada—as his meat of choice.

An aside here: Meat delivered to caterers offshore sometimes is difficult to identify. It's not so much the kind of meat; beef is always beef and pork always pork, and the outside wrapper says that. But the cut of the meat can be elusive. Sometimes the issue can be confused by skill and sleight of hand. One cook morphed some pork cutlets into "smothered beef" with several hours of oven braising and a thick, nearly black gravy that owed to an over-exuberance of Kitchen Bouquet. The morph may not have been intentional, and the stuff was weird, but tasty. It looked more like beef than pork, and no one complained. I was the one who asked what it was and was told, "Smothered beef. Well, it started out as pork but ended up beef."

Hamburgers and cheeseburgers are not included in the selection, and the catering crew, oddly enough, gets no credit for making and offering them every day. The "beef patties" item under meat dish is a hamburger patty, but it more resembles a "smothered beef patty" than it does the unfortunate and misnamed, but still iconic, "Swiss hamburger steak" of the Vietnam-era U.S. Army mess hall, Fort Dix, New Jersey. That was a generic ground meat patty covered in brown or black gunk. Offshore meat patties with onion and green pepper, Tony Chachere's, and a variety of spices are usually solidly OK, despite the possible disreputability of the ground meat.

One important meat product, that curiously didn't show on any of the lists above but played a central role offshore in the galley at all times and should be constantly kept in mind, is the corn dog. As previously mentioned here and elsewhere, the corn dog's role is fundamental, important, substantive, and contributory. Its absence from the roster of stars that particular week is an odd quirk, an ill-timed stroke of fate, and is in no way reflective of the superior stature of the corn dog offshore.

My reputation took a hit when the menu and circumstances disharmonically converged with a site visit by Taylors head honcho for drill rigs. Damning things to hell won't help, but it is worth observing that life has periodically slapped my face often when I deserved it, but occasionally not. My take-away lesson was and always has been that pride goeth before a fall. And I don't enjoy the fall, so I goes pretty easy on the pride. But sometimes it doesn't help, and I get wrung up anyhow. It's the Irish.

Marianas was a Taylors site. It was considered the best Taylors site, according to scuttlebutt, and it may have been one of the company's sites, surely one of the biggest drill sites. But the rig seemed demanding, fussy, and unfriendly. Whether it was Transocean, who owned it, or BP, who leased and ran it, I can't say for sure. But I'm thinking BP. Remember, this is the oil company that's going to fire your ass for pitching a cigarette butt into the ocean.

Being a lifelong free-marketeer, and worse, a food service peon, I believe the customer is right. Even if the customer is wrong, act like the customer is right, and do your best to make them happy and get shut of them. BP has the right to expect a certain level of service. It's what they're paying for and they're paying plenty. The Taylors operation on Marianas overall was OK. It did not consistently fail, but neither was it exemplary nor stellar. And therein might have been the difficulty.

The housekeeping was OK. The bedroom hands maintained the rooms—although some of the BP women found shortcomings in the maintenance of their rooms. Really? Women managers and bosses expressing dissatisfaction about the state of their quarters while doing a twenty-one-day hitch on an oil rig in the middle of the Gulf of Mexico? Goodness! One response to that might be: "Was it the housekeeping or was it the *room*?" Another, just as pertinent, more skeptical, yet perhaps more salient is: "Was it the housekeeping or was it the *job*?" In any case, they were bosses, and when bosses aren't happy, it's an unhappy time all around.

The laundry was good-to-very-good when Maria and Birdie were working regular shifts, and that was most of the time. The quality of the fill-ins might've fallen off—like me, for instance—but after a couple of get-it-together-and-learn nights, I was fast-tracking to do an acceptable job. A night or two of some confusion in the laundry shouldn't poison the well. If the confusion was a regular occurrence and lasted the entire time the regular crew was off, then that'd be just one more Unsatisfactory Check leading to take-a-hike land.

Perhaps, worst of all, the grub was OK. Some aspects, like salad and fruit bar and desserts were solidly good, especially when the main crew was working. Yet if you're looking for great grub on the line, the food fell short of the mark.

On July 4, I was still in the laundry and I decided

to chow down. The menu was extensive, as they always are on holidays offshore: steaks, baked potato, corn on the cob, boiled and fried shrimp, barbecue ribs, potato salad, cole slaw, hamburgers, hot dogs, and lots more, including a custom-made U.S.A. birthday cake. The cooks always take care to make the holiday meal special. It's a matter of personal pride for the catering staff, but also a break in the routine for the men because they're at work instead of at home with their families.

I sat down with the camp boss, a former chef with thirty years of experience, and a mighty big boy who once topped four hundred, but was now down to 320 and falling. I hadn't been eating too much, so I was pretty empty and had beaucoup space to fill. He had virtually unlimited capacity, and we packed it away. I ate mostly ribs, beans, a little potato salad, and cole slaw. And he ate everything.

It was OK. And *that* was the special effort.

Daily, it wasn't that the food was bad, but it didn't rise much above "industrial" quality. It reminded me of army grub in Europe, generally OK, and durable enough to satisfy hunger, but never quite rising to the level of "Good!" or better all along the line. A few selections, such as the hamburgers, were absolutely uninspired, mine included. Not much can be said in defense of a crew that can't make a tasty hamburger. Even if the cooking method is not ideal, precooked and then stored in liquid in a half pan on the grill, a professional should be able to figure out something that would salvage that most American of food items.*

---

*I think standardizing the serving size, the spices, the cooking procedures, and the storage methods would have resolved any issues. Once success was achieved in outcome through a short trial and error in recipe, prep, grilling, and warming, then the burgers wouldn't have been huge, random and various, overcooked, and desiccated.

Marianas

The red potato French fries we served up when we ran out of frozen were worse than uninspired, they were awful! The red potato is loaded with water and is dense and moist, unlike a russet, which is dry and grainy and the potato of choice for French fries in restaurants and commercial applications alike. It's theoretically possible to make a decent fry from a red potato in a mass-serving portion, but I've never seen it done. Even a CIA-trained chef who talked about twice-cooking them at two different temperatures, a technique that seemed correct in the jawboning, failed in execution. But I wasn't on deck when he made them, and I don't know if, in fact, he had time to twice cook them. On the line, they didn't seem like it, which made me think he didn't. And they were only marginally improved versions of the ones we schlumpfed up on Marianas. Ours were limp, lifeless, pale, and pathetic, and appropriately, not terribly popular!

Just a few more gigs leading to another Unsatisfactory Check.

Thinking about what wasn't right doesn't yield any quick or easy answers. The dayside cooks worked their tails off, so it wasn't lack of effort. They had a decent-sized crew, too, or so it seemed when they relieved me at 6:00 a.m. and flooded into the kitchen: main cook, assistant cook, kitchen helper/galley hand, salad bar specialist/galley hand, and one or two more galley hands doing dishes and maintaining the dining room.

Marianas just wasn't a happy rig. Maybe the expectations were high and the product delivery too low. The fact I was there, I believe, was symptomatic of the difficulties with the contract. I'm a decent cook, but I am not the world's most experienced cook. Putting a guy like me in the position of feeding 150 demanding mouths is a chancy proposition. I was up to it, and I showed improvement with each passing night, but the toll it took was considerable. After nine days, I was shot, physically done in, and glad to be relieved to the baker's bench.

I did nine days as cook instead of seven as cook and seven as baker because of Taylors staffing turmoil. The bedroom hand lead worker got whacked after a Sunday fire drill in which one guy was overlooked and not turned out. The body count did not match in the cafeteria staging area, and after a couple of re-counts that still did not add up, one of the BP guys went looking for the missing man and found him in the rack.

That is a mortal sin. During a fire drill, the catering bedroom hands are responsible for visiting each of their rooms, awakening the men, ensuring that they leave and that the rooms are empty. It's how the rig plans to be evacuated in an orderly manner in the midst of an emergency—men's lives are at stake—and there is no variance from the rule.

That performance exacerbated existing frictions, I believe.

Maybe the cooks' skill levels weren't what they should have been. One morning when I was new in the galley, James, the usual night cook working as baker, was helping me set out serving utensils in the last seconds before we opened the line. He sampled some of my grits and remarked, "Look at these grits. Nice and creamy. I wish my grits were like this." I was gratified for the kind words, but sort of taken aback. There is nothing special about making grits. You have to pay attention to them and taste them. It's something you boil, for Pete's sake! Add salt to the water, use a four-to-one ratio, and whip them occasionally with a whisk. I screwed up grits . . . once. The first night as cook on Herc 21, I didn't leave sufficient time to cook them, and when it came time for the line to open, they were still grainy, gritty, and undercooked. That never happened again. The fact James believed his grits weren't as good as mine I found revealing, and it bespoke more about the situation, perhaps, than was intended.

After the bedroom hand got whacked, tremors set out from the middle of the Gulf to catering central in La-fayette. A long talked about, unanxiously awaited, and fre-quently rescheduled site visit was laid on by the supervisor of drill rig operations for later that week. Wednesday was announced as the date at first, but that turned into Thursday. Mike, the supervisor, came aboard during the day, wearing a baseball hat that proclaimed SHERIFF. The camp boss sug-gested he take it off; Dodge was in good hands. It didn't need cleaning up as much as it did straightening out, and that was occurring without any additional firepower.

Mike's inspection seemed to confirm the assess-ment. The day was spent looking around and meeting with BP bosses and staff. I was in the rack and didn't see him until I came on and relieved dayside at 6:00 p.m.

The menu for the midnight meal called for chicken parmesan as the main dish, chicken strips as the alternate meat, and turkey patties as the meat dish. Though heavy on fowl, there was still sufficient variety of style to be accept-able. Mike was going to overnight on the rig and would be at the midnight meal.

Chicken or veal parm is a staple of Italian-American

cookery. It's a breaded cutlet—actually it's a bread crumb and finely grated parmesan cheese-coated cutlet—over which is poured a little marinara sauce, the whole then draped with a slice of melted mozzarella cheese. Like anything done right, it can be delicious. Restaurants with red and white checked tablecloths in Hartford, New Haven, Brooklyn, or Boston's North End offer it regularly and patrons gobble it up. Chicken or veal parm also adorns menus of commercial eateries and periodically fast-food stops across America, and those versions turn out variously from passable to halfway decent.

Because of Mike's visit, the menu called for some consultation. In looking it over with the camp boss, I'm told the chicken cutlets were used for something else and we're out. We re-jigger plans and come up with "turkey parmesan"—turkey patties from the meat dish slot promoted to main dish. I haven't used turkey patties before. In reconnoitering them, I find out they're frozen, breaded, and star-shaped. That's a clue that they're processed thingies, which doesn't make them "bad" as such, but "different." Sure, they could be one hundred percent plain ground turkey meat, but the fact they're shaped like five-pointed stars rather than patties indicates to me turkey meat parts and accessories extruded or stamped out under pressure.

The ubiquitous corn dog is promoted into "meat dish" status, but my notebook also has "bacon" next to it, which would be a truly bold, confident, potentially tasty, but naughty innovation, liable to elicit squeals of alarm from the American Heart Association.

The turkey patties get deep fried, so in plotting the meal, I take account of my new friend, the deep fryer, which will be making all three meat offerings as well as the plain

French fries.

I get my marinara going—diced onions and garlic in olive oil to start, whole tomatoes crushed by hand with their juice, parsley, basil, oregano, red pepper, tomato paste, Tony Chachere's, paprika, salt, and pepper to taste—and get on with it. Everything comes together pretty much as it's supposed to after three hours of non-stop hustle, and I open the line on time. The turkey parm tastes about like what you'd expect. An extruded commercial meat product over which is laced some decent marinara sauce then draped with a slice of mozzarella. It's OK. Not great. But OK.

I had a moment's indecision about how best to serve the turkey parm and decide to make two rows of ten patties each overlapping in a shallow pan. Figure two dozen servings per pan, I can keep the number of pans to a minimum. I place a slice of mozzarella on each patty and ladle a little sauce down the middle of the row thinking the cheese will melt with the heat of the patty and the extra sauce. I also ladle some sauce into the pan at the outside edges of the rows and down the middle just for color. I have the steam table on medium because I just want to keep them warm. The entrée looks OK. I've arranged the pan so the two legs of the stars are on the floor of the pan, the two arms in the middle, and the fifth point as a head. With the cheese and sauce, it looks inviting. And that's where the goodness stops.

It cannot be self-served easily. The same heat from the sauce on the patty's front that is helping to melt the cheese is also eroding the breading on the patty's back lying on top of it, having unanticipated chemical effects—like making super glue—and turning my entrée into a tangle of melted cheese and turkey patties with sauce slopped all over it and the line. Sometimes a serving will come away with the legs of the next turkey patty stuck to it. Sometimes long strings of cheese attach and will not surrender. Because the diners are holding their plates or trays, their hands are occupied and they are limited in their response to backing away or yanking at their portions to tug them free. This causes balance problems and precariousness issues while the cheese is unrelenting, adheres insanely, and laughs chillingly. Although no trays, plates, or patrons go down, it is a close-run thing. Gulf gravity, always a constant, but given to fickleness in inopportune circumstances on oil rigs, joins the fray at random, causing drops and occasional dollops of sauce to fall away to splash back into the pan loosing tomato sauce shrapnel on all. Gravity also causes whole sections and whole patties once or twice to stick together until the worst possible instant, then let go, free fall away from the diner's plate or tray and bounce, always designed to do the most damage to decorum, a clean set of overalls, and the orderliness of my line.

Mike and the camp boss come through the line before the festivities really get under way, but they're sitting with the bedroom crew at the caterers' table, which is the first table on the left, first table on the right looking out of the galley, and prime viewing overlooking the start of the line. I take executive command and pitch in, wielding another spatula decisively to quell the rambunctiousness and aid in the serving. It's not exactly a twisting, pushing, shoving knot of men fighting with the turkey parm, but it could be mistaken for one. Several guys grab trays and avoid the start of the line where the tussle is, and go over to where I'm not and start chirping for hambugers and cheeseburgers.

Attempting to convey grace under pressure, I am everywhere at the same time. I get on a load of fries. I whip off a quartet of burgers and wipe down the line from the outside. I dump the fries into their hole then reload my best friend with another batch of turkey patties, thinking I'll try a different set-up this time.

I notice Mike's plate and he's eaten one leg of the patty and his napkin covers the rest of the entrée. This will not do.

So I make him a fresh one on a new plate, cheese over the sauce, and run it into the oven for a few seconds to melt the cheese. I take it over to him. "This one is properly sauced," I say, removing his old one. It looks good but it's still a turkey patty parm and he doesn't eat that one either.

Later, after Mike left, the camp boss comes by and says, "Good marinara." Since he's not given to compliments, I take it as it came. He's right. It was good.

The visit results in more personnel change, all of which might have been planned or at least plotted before my arrival. The next day before leaving, Mike fires the dayside fill-in main cook and takes her back on the helicopter. James has a pretty strong reaction to this and quits the following day. His tenure might have been winding down anyway because we both came out the same time and I was told before setting off that the night cook job would be open in a week. He did his job for the week I was in the laundry, and as soon as Birdie returned and I was available, I was moved into his job and he got shunted off to baker.

He had pals on board because he had been there for a while, and they managed to get a chopper to take him off late afternoon despite the weekend. The camp boss calls me in to his office coming on shift, tells me what occurred, and says I'll be night cook until Mike can manage a replacement. Mike said he'd send out "a real cook," as he characterized it, to replace me. I was slightly annoyed, but what are you going to do when the boss doesn't like your grub, either from unfamiliarity or just plain dislike?

"That's fine," I reply, looking forward to my replacement and being able to observe "a real cook" in action because it occurred to me I hadn't seen any—at least any that were still employed—on Marianas so far.

The next night I made fried chicken and everything else, too, and it was the best meal I'd prepared to date. I got a couple of positive comments from the men, and just as importantly, I established my abilities to my own satisfaction.

Kevin came aboard and took over as night cook the next day. Kevin was a big old Lou'siana fella, a jolly, snoose-dipping brother just off a production rig. He knew his way around the galley. When Taylors wanted to reassign him from his rig, he said the men on the rig bitched to the boss who bitched to their company HQ who called Taylors and said "Unh-unh." Kevin stayed put for a number of additional months.

Marianas was finishing up its work for BP and was going to relocate by tow to the coast of South America the first part of August. Taylors was setting up the crew that would make the tow and Kevin was part of the package. Kevin's galley hand from the production rig formed his team and would be joining Marianas within the week. The galley hand would make the tow, too.

Kevin's transition from production cook to drill rig

night cook was a work in progress. The number of holes to fill on the line and the number of mouths to feed was a magnitude different from what he was used to. And having the line open a half-hour earlier than the posted dining room hours caused him confusion, too.

But everything could be summed up in one word: "Shee-it!" usually said breathily and with an exhalation.

"Shee-it" was Kevin's universal declarative. And it worked, too. As an exclamation, as a curse, as an expression of disappointment or annoyance, despair, good fortune, disbelief, agreement, joy, "shee-it" was there to affirm the occasion.

If the French fries were in too long: Shee-it.

If the French fries didn't go in on time: Shee-it.

If the line had to open in two minutes and nothing was ready yet: Shee-it.

If he had to lumber over to open the line: Shee-it.

One old doughboy attached to the 35th Missouri National Guard Division in World War I said of Capt. Harry S. Truman, "You never heard a man cuss so intelligently and so well." In Kevin's case, I never heard a man get such effective mileage out of a single cuss word!

The rest of the week for me was anticlimactic, toned down in physical demand and somewhat enjoyable as baker. A little excitement occurred at breakfast on my first day when the line opened. The camp boss came in and some little rat-faced booger went running over to him to bitch about the fruit bar not being open. Of course it wasn't open. Nobody did it. And the reason nobody did it was because *I* was supposed to do it and I didn't do it because I didn't know

I *had* to do it! Well, sort of. I did recollect James speeding around doing something on his own and passing repeatedly from the salad bar room through the galley into the dining room bearing trays of something, but as I was up to my eyeballs in last-minute hustle before the line opened. I can truthfully say I wasn't cognitively observing what he was doing. More likely I was pissed that he was off doing something on his own when I could use his damn help!

Anyhow, the camp boss came in and pointedly said I was responsible for the fruit bar, that it was supposed to open when the breakfast line did, and something like the bosses weren't happy when service didn't meet the stipulations of the contract.

Whoa, I thought, that's kind of a load to lay on a baker, as if I cared on the 19th day of a twenty-one-day hitch.

"I'm glad you told me," I responded. "I'll get right on it."

One last minor flap before I left that required counseling and instruction was when I didn't know how to cut a cantaloupe for the fruit bar. The stupidity derived from never using cantaloupe in commercial quantities. Even working for the Italian caterer in the late '60s I never prepared mass cantaloupe. Probably because prosciutto-wrapped cantaloupe was only just then, or had not yet, entered the American-Italian culinary landscape.

My usual method of procuring cantaloupe pieces was to cut a wedge, scoop out the seeds, and trim the fruit away from the rind. That works fine if you have all day to be dubbing around with individual servings. But there's a better way to get at it faster: Trim the rind and the green stuff off the whole fruit from the outside like you would an orange.

That way you're left with all usable material once you cut it in half and scoop out the seeds.

The camp boss was fuming at my ignorance, but the salad bar mistress was more patient and told me what to do. I thanked her and muttered something defensive about not needing commercial quantities of it previously. But that was stupid and puerile because I did need commercial quantities of it. I needed 'em fast, and I needed 'em now.

I guess a "real cook" would've known that.

The end came on a pretty Friday in late July. I didn't look back as we took off from the rig. I was damn glad to be off Marianas and was looking forward to a stint in Maine and a stint with a company other than Taylors.

Oh, and there was no sauna.

Back, but Gawd, just a shade of formerly
Friday, July 20, 2007 1:47 p.m.
From: "Patrick Keefe"
To: "Christopher Keefe"
Hiya Thuglee—

Gads!

Got here at 11:50. It's now 12:40. I unloaded the car and made a quesadilla with some savage (obviously local) habaneros and jalapenos and had a couple a Grolsches. No grub since last night (a trio of chicken wings and several cookies that I made—baker's tasting, of course!)

Work was basic training all over again. No sheee. It was sooo terrible, I'm damn near

161

quitting. In fact, I am quitting Taylors, but I'm taking six weeks or so off to recover, go to Maine, come back, then go to Fort Sill.

Oh, and the basic thang? Well, I wouldn't do Marianas again for anything, but the experience was priceless. I truly got beat to crap and in 2007, I'm not quite as resilient as I was in '71.

I'm betting I'm down to 175. For nine days I didn't eat—no time on shift. The rest of the time I slept. But boy, did I drink: water, Mountain Dew (full calorie), Kool-Aid, diet green Nestea®, pineapple and grape juice, and coffee. By the freakin' gallon.

Never saw the sun for twenty-one days. (I was on nights and didn't get outdoors.) Oh, and part of the take-away? I *really* am a good cook. That's not braggadocio; it's a damn fact. On Sunday, I made bloody good fried chicken for 140 plus people, filled ten holes on the serving line, including a pan of killer red beans and rice, opened on time, and got three compliments from the guys. All by my lonesome.

Three and a half hours later, I served seventy people breakfast, filled all the holes (scrambled, alternate scrambled with salsa) pancakes, French toast, bacon (140 pieces), links, sausage patties, home fries, red and white gravy (homemade), oatmeal, and grits. Plus eggs to order and omelets. For break-

fast we've only got to fill eight holes—the baker fills the last two. The guys liked that, too.

I was making $10 per hour. . . .

More later. Good to hear from yuz.

Careful Over There.

Love,

Pops

Gumbo

I love gumbo. In fact, since I moved to Lou'siana and started making it, gumbo has become one of my favorite "bowl" foods, seemingly intent on dethroning chili, my favorite bowl food. Chili has almost limitless virtues: taste, ease of making, versatility as breakfast, lunch, or supper, compatibility in tandem with eggs, salad, Texas toast, cornbread, or tortillas, plus sheer hunger-quenching power and other unspecified beatitudes. Gumbo may not have the versatility of chili—it's not as appealing for breakfast and doesn't go so well with black coffee—but what it lacks in morning utility, it more than makes up for in taste and texture.

Most gumbos offshore were served up Friday as part of Seafood Day. Naturally, they were mostly seafood gumbos with shrimp, oysters, and crabmeat. All were good. But I'm most partial to chicken and sausage.

Gumbo is slightly involved, although there are steps the experienced cook can take to minimize effort. But gumbo is best made when you have time, and it's superior on the day the LSU Tigers are playing football and you have some pals over to drink beer, listen to the pre-game show on the radio, and make a mess in the kitchen.

Cajuns just toss their chicken pieces, bones and all, into the gumbo. It works well and adds to the flavor. But I prefer not to have to be cautious when digging into gumbo and alert to ingesting bones, as well as frequently hauling them out of my mouth. I think it's easier on my guests, too. I use the chicken to flavor the stock, but then I pick it and use only the chicken meat in the gumbo.

I buy a four or five pound fryer and cut it in half and use half for stock and half for other things. I cut both halves into four pieces each: breast, wing, thigh, and drumstick. I cut the breast meat from the bones of the half I'm saving and add the bones to the stock pot. The drumstick, thigh, and wing I reserved I usually cook later on the grill. The breast meat I usually save for stir fry or quesadillas.

In making stock, sometimes I use a cheesecloth bag to hold the herbs, but not all the time. When I put them in loose, I strain the finished product twice. Once through a colander to catch the chicken and veggies, and then again through a strainer to catch the floating herbs. Toss out the veggies. They've given their all to make your stock fabulous.

Stock

6 quarts water
½ fryer chicken cut in four pieces
1 onion, quartered with skin on
4 carrots, broken in half and washed but not skinned
4 ribs celery, washed, broken in half, leaves on
2 cloves garlic, bruised
1 teaspoon parsley
1 teaspoon oregano
1 teaspoon basil
2 bay leaves
Tony Chachere's

Fill a pot with water. Add chicken, veggies, herbs, and spices and heat to boiling. Turn down to simmer. The chicken will be done after an hour. Leaving the stock on longer improves its flavor, but it can be ready in just sixty minutes if you're pressed for time. Remove chicken and pick meat from bones. Strain stock.

Roux

Roux is the foundation upon which gumbo is built. You want a delicious, deep, dark roux, "chocolate" or "brick red" in color. Cooks offshore, always short of time, frequently bake their roux. They mix one part fat to one part flour and bake it at 350 degrees up to two hours. If you bake yours, stir occasionally, and watch it closely as the time approaches two hours and the roux darkens.

Another way is to cook the same 1:1 ratio low and slow on the range. It's a little more hands-on, gives you greater control, and if you're obsessive, it will meet your personal anxieties better than stuffing it in the oven and forgetting about it. It's also faster than baking it, taking about an hour, although it doesn't allow you to concentrate on other things like baking does. Yet you can still get stuff done like knife work.

REDNECK *Gravy*

¾ cup oil
¾ cup flour

Mix together. Bake or cook on the range until dark brown or "red."

Gumbo
1 onion chopped
1 green pepper chopped
2 ribs celery chopped
3 cloves garlic smashed
2 quarts chicken stock
2 bay leaves
1 teaspoon Tony Chachere's
½ teaspoon cayenne
½ teaspoon dried thyme
salt and freshly ground black pepper to taste
picked chicken meat
1 andouille or smoked sausage cut into ⅓ inch pieces then quartered
2 cups rice
Optional (for garnish)
3 scallions cut thin
sprinkling of chopped parsley
filé powder

Heat your favorite stewpot over medium heat and add sliced and quartered sausage. Brown, stirring. The sausage will let off some fat and cook itself. Add onion, green pepper, celery, and garlic, and wilt. Add roux and chicken stock, bay leaf, and spices, and stir until roux is distributed. Turn heat down. Let it cook for 30 minutes. Add chicken. Taste and adjust seasoning. Make rice and drain.

I like filé and garnish on my gumbo, but some don't, so I usually make them available for guests to use as they see fit. Serve over fresh rice in a bowl with plenty of cold beer and crispy, fresh baguette.

CHAPTER 8

SONOCO

Returning to Baton Rouge after an absence that included two extended trips to New England, I thought I'd try my luck working for another catering company. I looked online and found SONOCO—once, the Sontheimer Offshore Catering Company—in Houma. They had been on my list the previous December when I was looking to break into the bidness, but I ended up with Taylors before investigating them further.

I drive to Houma—106 miles one way from Baton Rouge—but the round trips to New England I made had been more than 4,100 miles. So I was thinking, "What's a 212-mile round-trip between friends?"

I found the office, filled out the application, and was surprised to be offered a cook's written test then and there.

"Why not! It's what I'm here for."

So I proceeded to address that, too. The test was similar to Taylors—and I knew how important it was to fill in all the blanks. It wasn't that difficult, and there were only a couple of things that gave me more than a moment's pause, such as "How much baking powder do you use in biscuits made with 2 1/2 cups flour?" Well, a minimum of 2 1/2 teaspoons. But a lot of guys would argue with that and say two teaspoons per each cup of flour. The critical thing was to put something down.

A few minutes after I handed in the test, the human resources contact, Anthony, came out and told me I had passed. He asked when I was available for a cook's practical test, and I said I was flexible and could do it 'most any time.

He left, returned in about ten minutes and said, "Be here tomorrow at seven. You'll serve thirty or forty."

That was fast! But why not? I asked to see the galley and was taken across the lot from the office to the warehouse building and up to the second level. I nosed around, and it looked like a dining room and galley, but I think the speed with which things were happening, and the fact I was committed to returning in less than sixteen hours and making a meal, tipped me into sensory overload, or just plain stupid. Afterwards, I recalled only a little of the recon and nothing about the kitchen set-up. I did not, for instance, remember there was a homeowner model four-burner electric stove in the kitchen. In fact, I did not recall seeing a stove at all!

I asked what I would be preparing and the response was purposefully vague; you know, the sort of meal served offshore. A couple of main entrees, breads, and dessert. "Shrimp Creole" entered my head from somewhere, although whether from a menu planner I saw by mischance, or from someone else I met in the know, I do not recall.

I reviewed shrimp Creole from Chef John Folse's Cajun grub encyclopedia and it's easy enough: add shrimpies and tomatoes to a Cajun trinity (onions, bell pepper, celery). I looked over pie crust and thought about bread recipes, but put them off because any bread I ever made offshore was from a package mix, and I'm going to be making an offshore-style meal.

I counted backwards from when I was supposed to arrive, 7:00 a.m., and that figured into a wake-up at 4:30 a.m. and on the road at 5:00 a.m. And that's how it went.

Up and at 'em, shower, and make a thermos of Starbuck's French roast, then into Blackie Jr. and down to Houma. Crossing the I-10 bridge over Lake Pontchartrain was no problem, and after drifting southwest on I-310, I pulled into Houma right around 7:00. I went to the office and was again taken up to the galley/dining room in the warehouse.

I got the menu, met the woman, Margaret, who cooked for the warehouse gang daily—she'd be "observing" me and helping out, but only in locating things. I was on my own for cooking.

It was going to be a busy morning. I was going to make:

Menu item

beef stew	shrimp Creole
dirty rice	turnip greens with diced turnip
two-crust pie	field peas with diced green beans
bread	biscuits

None of the items by themselves presented a problem. I make tasty beef stew. I was up to speed on shrimp Creole. There's a lot of slicing and dicing—garlic, green peppers, onion, tomato—but I'm fast with a knife. I did not have to clean the shrimps. No problem. Dirty rice, OK. Usually it's made with chicken livers, which I despise, but there weren't any, so Margaret suggested I used leftover hamburger. Fine. With some chicken stock and seasoning, no problem. Turnip greens and turnip turned out to be frozen veggies and the field peas were canned, so no problem.

The pie, bread, and biscuits were not problems, either, because I decided to act professionally. As I do coming on shift anytime offshore, I brought along to SONOCO my cook's "attaché" case (an Albertson's plastic bag) in which I had my cap, cutting glove, nicely faded LSU Tiger/camouflage apron, three timers, insta-read thermometer, knife sharpener, Wüsthof-Trident eight-inch chef's knife, razor sharp Chinese cleaver, Sharpie and adhesive tape for marking and dating leftovers, pen, notebook, and my copy of *Culinary Arts Institute Encyclopedic Cookbook*. I do not carry around the recipes for homemade biscuits or pie in my head. I don't have to. Offshore, biscuits are made out of a bag, and many pies come from a pre-made or frozen crust and a can of filling.

If I need a recipe, I look it up in my book. And that's what I did here and why I was feeling confident.

But . . . just as individually none of the items presented a problem, collectively they presented a helluva problem. Bread, pie, *and* biscuits? Cripes, that's a minimum of two-and-a-half or three hours in the oven baking right there. The only thing I'm catching a break on is the freakin' frozen and canned veggies, and both of them are going to present cook-top issues later.

It was 7:37 a.m. when I learned what my menu was. Lunch was on for 11, meaning I had three hours and twenty-three minutes to do this. Thinking about it came off *my* time.

It took about eleven minutes to cogitate over and

work out a plan and timetable and then it was Slam It! time. Before I began, I asked about food prep gloves and was astonished to learn, "There aren't any."

I didn't go into detail like: "What do you mean? There aren't any right now? Or there aren't any ever?" But considering the galley/dining room was on top of a warehouse that presumably supplied SONOCO catering crews with groceries and supplies throughout the Gulf, the lack of gloves wasn't questionable as much as it was head-shakingly incomprehensible. Damned dangerous, too, if an inspector should show up or blow in.

I enjoyed the retro freedom, like "wet-finger dentistry" of the '70s, and put the issue out of mind immediately.

Bread and pie were the first priorities because the bread had to rise and would take an hour to bake. Pie crust was next because my recipe called for it to chill. I used the recipe for "white bread straight dough method" from the cookbook and got the milk on to scald as I prepped the yeast. Following directions, the rest came together pretty quickly, and in only a few minutes, I had a nice bowl of dough ready to rise.

Pie crust came next. I'm not really "afraid" of pie crust—there's nothing to be afraid of—but I have little experience with it. There's some history here. I was hooked early and young on cigarettes. Think single digits. I believe the addiction to nicotine changed my body chemistry before my body had a chance to build up to and assert its All-American indestructibility. The change—defect—expressed itself in a weird chemistry that produced overwhelming stomach acidity after consuming some foods—Dunkin' Donuts and pie, chiefly. This was a sad happenstance since Dunkin' Donuts was one of the first places to be open twenty-four hours a day. No matter, my physical reaction restricted my consumption of what otherwise would have been a typical New England commitment to Dunkies morning, noon, and night. Tums worked later in life to quell the acidity, but ten-year-olds in the early '60s could get cigarettes easier than they were likely to understand the relationship of Tums to that creepy stomach feeling! As far as pie went, I avoided it, limiting myself to having a couple pieces of mince meat at Thanksgiving. And there were always baleful results in the aftermath.

Following directions, working quickly, and keeping everything cold, the pie crust came together in short order, and I wrapped it in plastic and popped it into the fridge. Margaret and I carried on a conversation sporadically while I was cooking. She was very helpful when I couldn't find something, reacting quickly to aid me. She kept busy keeping my pots and pans washed and doing other tasks, although I don't know what because I was concentrating on my own stuff. She did say in the course of the conversation she was a big fan of *This Old House* on public television, and she was excited about telling her family that she spent the day with a guy who talked just like the guys on the show. "They really do talk like that!" she said with authority after witnessing it in person.

I chuckled but didn't bother to explain that, no, I didn't sound like them; I speak the King's English and they're just a bunch of "Massholes." She seemed like a good Christian Cajun lady, and I didn't think she'd understand the nuance!

I started the beef stew next, cutting the meat, flouring it, and getting it on to brown in batches. I finely diced the onions, and when the meat was done, I swapped it out to sauté the onions and a little garlic. I peeled and cut the potatoes and carrots to have them ready, and when the onions were wilted, I returned the meat to the pot, added some Tony Chachere's, Worcestershire, paprika, cayenne, salt and pepper, and enough water to cover the ingredients. When the liquid boils, I'll add the potatoes and carrots and turn the heat down to a simmer.

Bread next. I punched down the dough although it hadn't risen too much. The galley was air conditioned, of course, and I think the temp was too cool for it to rise the way I would have liked.

Time was marching right along, so I started on my pie. I used the Formica-like counter as my work bench and the bottom crust went down fine. The top crust of my mandatory "two-crust" pie was a bitch to get up without ripping after rolling, despite what I thought to be appropriate applications of flour, so I chiseled and cut the rolled and stuck crust into strips and laid them into a lattice. "Fancy will be my top crust," thought I speaking English like Louis L'Amour wrote cowboy books. The strips were somewhat more manageable than the whole tearing top, but in the end it worked OK and looked halfway decent. I jazzed up the canned apple filling with lemon juice, more sugar, and cinnamon, and it was decent, too. In went the pie to a hot oven.

Yow! Looking down after clean-up, the Formica-like workbench top bore three dozen scars from where I cut the lattice. True, I was using a knife that was sharp as hell, but I was also cutting pie crust for Pete's sake, not anything I was leaning into. I didn't anticipate it happening, nor did I think it should have. Not because I didn't use a cutting board, but I figured a work surface in a commercial kitchen would've been more cut resistant than it was. Annoyed and cognizant that the SONOCO people might've been a tad unhappy to have their counter top permanently scarred, I made sure I kept a cutting board over the hack marks.

I put on some rice to get going on the dirty rice, and then I worked on the Creole shrimp. As I was finely slicing some garlic, I shaved the middle part of my left middle fingernail right off. That was stupid because I shouldn't have been using my nail as a guide; I should have used my knuckles and kept the knife's edge below them. It hurt, but not too badly, and there was no blood. So I kept on going, and damn if the very next cut, I didn't do the exact same thing again. This time I shaved off a thicker slice, drawing blood, and having it sting like the devil. "Fast" with a knife is not always synonymous with "good."

I couldn't believe how stupid I was. I also had two thoughts: Dripping blood into the Creole shrimp is a fireable offense. So too is cutting without your cutting glove, which you wear whenever you're doing knife work so that you *don't* cut yourself.

"Geez, I'm going to get whacked before I even get hired. . . ."

Fortunately, Margaret was elsewhere so the first aid went unobserved. I dug through my attaché Albertson's bag, took out the adhesive tape, pulled off a three inch long, half-inch wide strip, and wrapped it around my finger.

That seemed to serve, but we'll see. Some gloves would help hide the wound, too, but not on this caper.

The pie came out redolent in its glory, GB & D, golden brown and delicious, as Food Network's Alton

Brown exclaims, fragrant apple/cinnamon steam billowing upwards. Hell, that sucka looked and smelled good enough all by its lonesome to make the hire a done deal. It also made me want a piece, although I had no Tums or Rolaids in my attaché bag.

I turned the oven down from pie-high-heat, collected my bread dough, lubed the bread pans and put them in to bake. If it turned out anywhere near as good as the pie, then, Hoo-Wah!

I reserved half the rice for just plain white rice to go along with the shrimp Creole. Dirty rice, with meat, seasoning, and spices, has a distinctive flavor that, to my mind, does not complement the flavors of the shrimp. As an accompaniment? Perhaps. But surely not as a base over which you pour the shrimp medley. So there will be two kinds of rice.

The dirty rice is good. I crumbled up Margaret's left over burger, and I found some breakfast sausage odds and ends to dice, brown up, and include. With some Tony Chachere's, some finely-diced onion, chicken stock, and a little bit more tinkering, the rice is tasty, and the color is brown like "dirty" rice usually is. I'm right on target there.

I'm also approaching the lunch hour. Margaret and I go over how we'll set up the line. She has chafing dishes she uses routinely and I decide on main trays of shrimp and stew, flanked by a main tray with both rices, and after the stew goes a main tray of the two veggies. It looks neat and balanced, but it also looks sparse. The bread will help. I plan on artfully wrapping it in a dish towel and placing it on a cutting board with several slices cut and arranged.

I decide a small salad will help, too, so I cut some

iceberg, dice a tomato, add some croutons and Parmesan, salt and pepper, and dig out a collection of dressings.

This is looking smart!

I still have to do the biscuits, but I'm prepared for that. The bread comes out at about 10:45, and it looks like perfect loaves of country bread.

Damn, I'm good!

I coax one out of the pan and set it on the rack to cool down. Wouldn't dare try to slice it now.

I'm short of space on the range, so I live dangerously and dump the canned peas into the chafing dish and set the dish on high. They'll heat up in the pan. The frozen stuff I've got bubbling away on the range.

The stew is ready, so I put it out. It tastes good. The shrimp Creole is delicious, and I put that out too.

The biscuits are from scratch, so I fork in some butter and use some buttermilk Margaret had in the fridge instead of water or milk. I scatter some flour on the counter, dump the dough out, pat it down four times, and cut the biscuits out with her donut cutter. They go into a hot oven for fifteen to eighteen minutes at 10:59 a.m.

I'm very close.

Working like Marianas night cook now, that is to say, feet barely touching the ground, I drain the turnip and greens in a colander over a pot. I dump them into the half pan for the chafing dish and add back just enough liquid. I slice off a big chunk of butter and throw it on top. Over to the line.

I take the bread, cut off four slices, and cut them in half and fan them out. The bread looks like the country/farmhouse loaf it is. The crumb is coarse and the big, rounded, brown crust is pretty. We'll see. I take a plastic bowl, open a couple of paper napkins to act as doilies, and dump in a mix of butter patties and individual margarine servings. Placed next to the bread, it looks inviting and costs maybe forty-five seconds.

I try the field peas and they're warm. Not hot. "Marginal," thinks I.

Everything's down except for the biscuits. It's 11:02 a.m. and there are four or five waiting to go through the line. Hell yeah!

I sing and dance. I invite them in and introduce myself and Margaret. She blushes. I tell them what's for lunch, pointing at each dish. I 'fess up over the biscuits, but inform them they'll be out in ten or twelve minutes. I suggest they hold off on their pie until they've finished their meal, which of course includes biscuits, so stand by.

They chuckle. Then they eat.

When the biscuits are done, I put a few out on a rack, just to get them out there and announce, "Hot fresh biscuits, he-ah," as I always do. The others I let cool for a few minutes, then make a tray and put them on the line next to the bread and butter.

Lunch rolls on while I observe the line and putter about in the kitchen. Several gangs of workers and two tables of bosses come through. I'm not displeased with how things went. But I am sort of tuckered. It's the let down from an hours-long high energy commitment that began really at 4:30 a.m. when I rolled out.

Several folks stop by and compliment us on the meal. I say "us" because I always included Margaret in acknowledging their comment. The meal wouldn't have come out the way it did without her. It's always nice when some-one speaks well of your effort. It's nicer when a Cajun from Houma compliments your Cajun fare. None other than Mar-garet said the shrimp Creole was "very good." High praise, indeed, from someone who cooks for a living and makes the dish for her family. Nicer yet is when one of the bosses flat out asserts my biscuits "were the best she'd ever had." This was a real Southern lady. Even if she wasn't a Louisiana na-tive, she was a Southerner, and she would've had a lifetime's exposure to biscuits. Of course she could've been lying, but why? I'm taking her at her word. (In fact, afterwards I tried one and they *were* good. Still warm, flaky, and flavorful.)

Both pies got eaten, so that speaks for them!

After the meal and before clean-up, Kent, the food boss, comes by for a critique. He says the field peas were only lukewarm. And he's right. He said the stew juice was thin at first, but in looking at it after being in the chafing dish for a while, it had thickened considerably. He's right, there, too. My stew juices (and chili and gravies) are thin rather than thick. That's not to say watery, but they're not something you fork into your mouth. I prefer it that way. I can add heft to a stew—with flour if there's time to cook or a slurry of cornstarch and water if time's short. It's easier than trying to repair something thick, dense, and possibly clumpy. But I need to consider this fundamentally, maybe look more closely at the viscosity during cooking. In any case, fair critique and good observation. He said the bread was rough and needed to rise again. And he's right there, too. But considering the circumstances, I was satisfied with a country loaf rising once in a cool atmosphere and being on the line at lunch time rather than a perfect loaf showing up after the gang had eaten.

All in all, he said, it was a good meal, things were flavorful, and I was hired. I thanked him. He said I should go see the human resources guy in the office, and then I was done for the day.

I said OK. He left, and I set to help Margaret finish breaking down and cleaning up. There were a couple of biscuits left, and she took them along with the remaining bread. I don't know for sure, but that bread looked like it would have made fantastic toast. It reminded me of Cushman's Homestyle when I was a kid.

I traipsed over to the office from the warehouse/galley, saw Anthony, and told him what Keith said. He nodded and said he had a safety test for me to take. I acquiesced—it turned out to be similar to the one I took for BP and Marianas, and the test is based on common sense and a few concerns special to offshore work.

I finished it, he took it and graded it—I passed—then he said we were all done for the day. I should come back at 8:00 a.m. Monday, we'd do some insurance and other forms, get uniforms, and finish up the hiring process.

So Monday I returned. My first form was for health insurance, and I filled it out and passed it in. A couple of minutes later, he called out from his office and said, "Can you come in here?"

"Sure." I went in and sat down.

"I can't hire you," he said.

I was sort of surprised, especially since his boss told me I was already hired after lunch on Friday.

"Why not?" I queried. "I've been offshore and I'm

cleared for work."

"No man," he said. "Insurance will never go along."

"Why wouldn't they?" I said somewhat more point-edly. "I've already *been* offshore. I'm cleared for work. My bypass surgery was years ago; doctors have signed off on it. You have my physical and medical records right there. Put it through and let's see what happens."

He was unconvinced but allowed that he'd try. And he'd let me know.

A Yankee I met who moved to Louisiana a decade ago said one of her most important lessons, and one of the most aggravating traits, she found here was the lack of fol-low-up.

I know what she means.

From e-mail:

Cook on hold

Wednesday,September 26, 2007 7:25 a.m.

From: "Patrick Keefe"

To: "Personnel"

Good morning, Anthony.

I trust no news is good news!?

If there's any other documentation you need to affirm our case, just let me know.

Regards,

Pat Keefe

Night cook on hold—insurance
Monday, October 8, 2007 3:57 p.m.
From: "Patrick Keefe"
To: "Personnel"

Hello Anthony—

I thought I'd check to see if SONOCO's insurance company had a chance to review my stress test/health folder.

I'm still interested in working for the company.

I know you're extremely busy, so just give a call when it's convenient for you.
Regards,
Patrick Keefe

And three phone call messages plus fourteen months later and counting, I've still not heard back from him. I'm no expert in labor law, but it seems if you're hired, you're hired. It also seems if you're hired then something comes up that makes the hire objectionable—you know, age, or medical status, or race, or creed, or something—then as an employer, you have an obligation to discuss that with your employee— the guy you hired!

But not in my case.

I just figured in the case of SONOCO, "old guys need not apply."

Shrimp Creole

Order shrimp Creole in a restaurant in south Louisiana and it's bound to be good. But what kind of Creole you'll get remains to be seen. There are as many versions of it as there are Cajun and Creole enthusiast cooks. Some use a roux; some don't. In this version, I don't. But I do use head-on shrimp that I peel and clean myself because I use the shells and head to make the dish's sauce.

To decapitate a shrimp, grab him and twist his head off. Careful how you go about it. Shrimps have a bony proboscis that can (and will) stick in your hand, making tiny holes that sting and bleed. Do it enough and it's aggravating. Throw the head in the pot along with the shells, two quarts of water, and some Tony Chachere's. Bring to a boil, then turn down heat and simmer for 30 minutes or so. Strain and use the liquid in your dish.

I always remove the entrails from my shrimp. Yes it is a pain in the butt, both for you and for the shrimp, especially if you're doing four or five pounds of twenty-count shrimp. But I figure my guests deserve it. Cleaning them also diminishes the esoterics of your shrimp. Shrimp with tails on look great, but it's damnably hard to preserve the tail and remove the poop chute, so in the scheme of things, off comes the tail.

This might be New England fastidiousness learned from eating lobster and taken to a fault. A lobster has a notable entrail in the tail that requires removal. That requirement applied to shrimp might be regional *de rigeur* gone awry. I've never bitched about being served tail-on shrimp, but I'm careful about eating them. Yet neither do I ever recall being praised for serving up meticulously clean shrimp.

2 pounds peeled and deveined shrimp; save shells and heads to make stock.
2 tablespoon olive oil
1 onion chopped
1 green pepper chopped
2 ribs celery sliced thin
2 cloves garlic smashed
Tony Chachere's

SONOCO

2 bay leaves
½ teaspoon cayenne
hot sauce to taste
2 cups fresh tomatoes, seeded and diced
2 cups shrimp stock
Salt and black pepper to taste
2 cups rig rice

Garnish
2 scallions thinly sliced
Sprinkle of parsley

Heat pot over medium and add olive oil. When at temperature, add onions and sauté. When translucent, add green pepper, celery, and garlic. Sauté. Add tomatoes, Tony Chachere's, spices, bay leaves and cook. Add shrimp stock to cover the cooking veggies and let cook for five minutes. Taste. Add shrimp and cook just until they're pink. They go fast, so do not overcook! Add salt and pepper to taste.

Garnish and serve over rice.

CHAPTER 9

Mexico

After the Sonoco fiasco, I was let down. During the application process, and particularly after the cook-off, I had hallucinations of me in different circumstances on further adventures. Helicopter flights and crew boats to new and different rigs. New guys from the company and the crew to meet and befriend. Fresh situations, both good and stressful, to experience.

There I was, whipping up breakfast for a smartly turned out crew, in a bright, shiny galley on a classy and squared away rig. Sonoco's uniform of khaki slacks and a white short-sleeve polo shirt offered an improved visual style of raiment over Taylors utility hand prison blues. Although the white polo for a cook seemed to be a dicey proposition—more likely, a self-annihilating prophecy. After a couple of shifts, and despite washing grease, grime, gravy, tomato sauce, and bean juice splashes, not to mention blood and just plain dirt, it seems certain the shirt would morph from the stylish into the movie caricature of ship's cook, stained skivvy shirt straining over huge pot belly.

Disappointed, but far from bereft, the thought process was simple and went something like: "I need to get back to work. How about Taylors?"

So I called up dispatch and asked about assignments.

"Where have you been?" the dispatcher asked, sounding a bit miffed. "We tried to get hold of you, but there was no answer. We never heard from you, so you're not on the employment roster anymore."

"I've been out of state," I reply. "I had to go to New England, and there was personal business I needed to attend to. I didn't check in because I wasn't here and was unavailable."

"Well, you don't work here anymore," the dispatcher said. "You'll have to get reinstated."

This proved more nettlesome than anticipated, but not, in retrospect, unexpected. I drove over to Lafayette and submitted an application again. I was told to go to occupational medicine, where they checked over my records and said I needed . . . a stress test.

Best occupational medical practices being what they are, the two months I was absent could mean anything to them, I guess: maybe suffer a heart attack (and recover sufficiently to go back offshore); or undergo additional surgery (ditto); or become addicted to something then get clean. In any case, I found myself back at Louisiana Cardiology in Baton Rouge, checking in with Dr. Moraes, and setting up the test.

I don't like stress tests. It's not the "stress." I'm well aware of Louis L'Amour's and Jack London's dictum that "the legs go first." And after several stress tests now, I am acutely conscious of just how non-durable my legs are. After nine minutes on the treadmill accelerating and increasing the incline every two minutes, the old gams are aching, and after eleven minutes, I'm ready to quit. Then there's the creepy feeling of the ticker pounding at max rate, staggering off the machine onto a gurney, laying there breathing hard, sweating and smelly, unable to walk it off, while comely medical assistants observe and move the sensor around your chest.

OK. It is the stress.

But this one passes with no more than mild discomfort, burgeoning resentment over approaching geezerhood, and a deepening inkling of decrepitude. The results are pretty good, considering. After several days, I have them in hand and return to the occupational medical fortress in Lafayette. One of the assistants recalls me from the initial flap over surgery and stress tests the past winter. If she's not glad to see me, I imagine I'm in her prayers for survival, or at least that she won't find me in front of her on a highway somewhere, poking along at a rollicking thirty-five in a fifty-five mph zone and no place to pass. The little jezebel.

With pee test negative and glowing cardiology results, I'm approved again for duty and take the paperwork back to Taylors. My water and safety certification credentials are still in order, and I renew friendship with the personnel clerk/logistician Ramona and with Ralph, the new safety guy. They ask if I'm interested in a six-week posting in Arizona baking for two thousand, and I reply that's a little ambitious. Then they ask if I have a passport and unthinkingly, I respond "Yes."

"Want to take a rig to Mexico?"

"Not really," I think, but manage to say, "What's it all about?"

"We need a night cook/baker. The rig is in Texas being refitted, and then it's going to be towed to the Pemex fields off Campeche. The trip will be a couple of weeks, possibly twenty-one days."

"It's a Hercules rig?" I ask. I like Hercules rigs, despite seemingly all of them being elderly rust-buckets.

"Yes."

"Well sorta," might have been a better answer. It turned out the rig is a Todco rig. Hercules Offshore acquired Todco, a rival drilling company, in a two-billion-dollar-plus deal the previous spring. I was aboard Hercules 11 when the deal went through and wondered what the hell the "Taco" company was that had all the Hercules tongues wagging. I later came to understand the magnitude of the coup and how in the offshore world, the deal could be likened to Burger King buying out McDonald's. My Yankee ears never did understand how "Todd-Co" came to be pronounced "Taco," but it is.

The thought process evaluating an offer to take a rig somewhere is a checklist. It goes quickly something like:

1. Mexico. I like Mexico. Check.
2. Duration. Three weeks tops. That's getting out there, but it's not too long. Besides, you've been off two months now, OK. Check.
3. Leaving from a new port in Texas. It's an adventure for sure. OK. Check.
4. Being towed at sea. Ahhh, cripes. You could be seasick and there's nothing worse than that. True, but you always got your sea legs before and, besides, how rough can it get? Sure the

idea of cooking when seasick is so repellent as to nearly make me vomit right there, but the cooler half of the head prevails and asserts, "Listen, if you're sick, most everyone else will be, too, so no one will be eating. Think cruise ship. And even if you get a little queasy, think adventure." OK. Check.

"OK. It sounds like an adventure. What do I have to do?"

Their relief is palpable.

First they need to do paperwork with the consulate in New Orleans, so they need my passport. I'll bring it tomorrow, I say. They also ask about uniforms, and I reply that I was never issued more than utility-hand togs. So they take measurements for chef's pants, and, the uniform having changed, they take my shirt size. Red polos with a Taylors insignia on the left chest for all hands; cooks wear chef's checked pants; and utility hands still wear inmate blue Dickies.

I return the next day and turn over my passport. Mexico being a sovereign country, they control their borders rigorously. Since I'll be working there, I need a green card. I get a couple of updated passport photos from a nearby Walgreen's and I don't bother thinking too much about the irony of Mexican border control on the Mexican side of things. I'm not too keen on letting my passport go, but I have no need to flee or abscond, and I'm not planning for a weekender in Paris, so what th' hey?

I also get a briefing, most of which I forget until later when I recall it with chagrin at what they said.

Not surprisingly, the info is enough to operate on and no more. Offshore catering is like that. The shipyard is in Ingleside, Texas. I'm to find the "Keywitt" or "Kiewitt" dock and the boat "Bayou Blue." I'm responsible for getting there, and I should report at 6:00 a.m. Sunday. They ask me to bring some supplies—towels, mostly—and I should call the dispatcher when I'm an hour out of Lafayette to rendezvous en route.

Because I'm hauling supplies, I'm getting mileage. And I'm surprised to look online and learn Ingleside isn't near Houston or Galveston about four-and-a-half hours drive from Baton Rouge, but outside of Corpus Christi, nearly five hundred miles and eight hours driving time. Whoa!

That changes a lot because I'm too old and precious to drive all night and then go on shift. Needless to say, overnight accommodations aren't offered, so this one is on me. I figure I'll leave at 10:00 a.m. Saturday and get in around 6:00 p.m. That'll allow for a decent supper and a little exploring. I make tentative arrangements with the dispatcher to meet him around 11:00 a.m. Saturday at the office and pick up the cargo.

Saturday is a perfect south Lou'siana fall day. I meet the guy in Lafayette, get my load, and hit the road again. I enjoy the trip. In Houston, I'm a little taken aback when, on the Sam Houston Parkway, I'm stopped about every mile or two and have $1.50 or $2 extracted from me in toll. I've got good credit, but not so much cash, and the $14 or $16 taken from me is unexpected. I pass through that vale of toll a wiser, but poorer, man. The plan is to take Texas 59 southwest from Houston to Victoria, then Route 77 to the outskirts of Corpus Christi. There's Texas football on the radio, the sun is out and shining brightly, the landscape is large and infinite, and all's going well. I stop and refuel in Victoria and head out again. In Vidauri, I push in the clutch to upshift and something is amiss. The pedal stays down. Aggravated but not alarmed, I reach down and pull it back. Clutching again to shift, the pedal stays down and I'm unable to easily engage the shifter. I pull the clutch back again, but the pedal is unresponsive. Now I'm alarmed. It's going on 5:00 p.m., I'm at least an hour out of Corpus, and that doesn't include fiddling around to get to Ingleside. After a few moments of trial and error, I realize my five-speed transmission automobile is without a clutch.

It's not a disaster, but it's pretty damn close. Although I don't panic, there's a serious hormone dump and my heart starts thumping, blood pressure rises, curses roll easily off the lips, ordinary ruddy Mick complexion metamorphoses into a glowing red giant with equally as great chance of terminal explosion.

Owning a Saab is similar to matrimony. It's expensive; love plays a fleeting role; but respect is necessary and constant. In exchange, the vehicle will move you reliably from Point A to Point B at a safe speed and treat you well on fuel consumption. Occasionally, if need be, it can hurtle along with hair-raising dispatch.

The squeals, groans, grinds, squeaks, and screams the car emits as I continue driving and shifting without a clutch add to my discomfort. At stop lights, I learn to press the shift so that the gears are touching and slowly get under way before whamming into second gear to gain momentum. Several times I stall. Folks behind me are unhappy as I begin to move, but hardly accelerate. Many honk, and probably

191

most are thinking "Lou'siana asshole!" I know I would—but I have my four-way flashers on and there's obviously something wrong.

Required by training and custom to follow the army dictum of "don't do nothing," I stop at an O'Reilly Auto Parts store. It's coming on dusk and they're near to closing, but the clerk is a true motorhead and interested in the problem. I've had clutch cables go before, and that's how I diagnose the problem. He tells me Saab parts have to be ordered in Texas, but a pal of his is a Saab enthusiast and backyard wrencher, and he calls him to improve his knowledge base. The pal replies parts do have to be ordered and the more esoteric parts take longer. He adds there is a dealer in San Antonio, about 150 miles from Corpus Christi.

It's not necessarily good, but now at least I know what I'm dealing with. The hormone dump has receded, and I'm getting the hang of smashing my beautiful car around without a clutch. Finally arriving on the outskirts of Corpus Christi, I try to minimize my pointless wandering and consult the map to get to the shipyard expeditiously. But I miss a turn and enter the city proper. Exiting requires some back and forth in the dark and deserted industrial part of town on Saturday night. I make more than one California rolling stop at unpopulated stop signs, my head swiveling nervously as I pass furtive shadows of bums and Morlocks just awaiting a chance to rip out and eat the heart of a guy who can't even shift his car without grinding gears like a juvie skateboarder in a stolen Maserati. I recross the bridge over the bay, exiting the highway for local streets in Ingleside. Continuing to "don't do nothing," I finally stop at a convenience store that I know beforehand will be useless. Expectations met, I am paid off handsomely in both stupidity *and* futility. But with foresight, I park on a slope to roll backward because I can't get the car into reverse. Having failed illustriously to get the information I need, I set out to canvas Ingleside. After more than an hour of quartering town, I end up at a guard shack with armed Marines providing security for the naval facility. I tell them what's what: I'm stupid; I can't find what I'm looking for; I barely know what I'm looking for; and I don't have a clutch. Although they don't know for certain where I'm supposed to be, they think I should try one industrial plot over. I head out to the main road, turn left, take the first left again and drive down.

This looks promising. Intense, industrial power white and yellow-orange sodium vapor lamps light the sky and illuminate a large area. There's a huge fenced parking lot on the left and steel buildings ahead. Numerous crane derricks sprout here and there. To the right approaching the gate shack, there's a fancy stone building with pennants flying, the design indicating recent construction and considerable capital. At the gate shack, I stop. In the background an enormous, multideck production platform under construction drips glowing embers from uncounted welders at work, and the legs of a couple of jack-up rigs stand equally as tall. I leave the car running, get out, stretch, and repeat my tale of woe to the guards.

"Evening. I'm Patrick Keefe from Taylors. I'm supposed to relieve the night cook/baker on Taco 250. I'm looking for the Kiewitt Dock. The dispatcher said I should find the MV Bayou Blue."

The guards look at me.

"Dunno 'bout no boat Bayou, but Taco 205 here,"

one says.

The numbers are different, and there's no acknowledgement of the "Kiewitt" dock, which turns out subsequently to be the Kiewit Company, but it's close enough.

"OK. I'm supposed to report at 6:00 a.m. tomorrow, but I've got some towels that I think they need, and some other stuff. I can bring them over."

"You can drop them here," the other says. "We'll call and have them delivered. You come back tomorrow morning. Park over there," he says, indicating the lot. "We'll take you over."

I tell them my clutch is gone and I don't have reverse, so I have to enter the complex, turn around, and exit. They're OK with that, and they open the gate on the other side.

So it's nine o'clock on Saturday night in Ingleside. Things didn't quite work out as I had forecast, but I've found my destination and dropped off my cargo. I know where I need to be and how to get back. Now it's time to lay me down. In quartering the town, I spotted a Comfort Inn on the main drag. I head back there and take a room. I park Blackie Jr. on a slight incline so I can roll out of the space in the morning. Being an experienced traveler, and having lived more than a day in parking lots awaiting transport offshore, I'm well armed for eventualities. I've got a sandwich and chips, peanuts, crackers and cheese, hot peppers in a baggie, and a Playmate with a clutch of Grolsch beers.

The room is a standard Comfort Inn. I shower to wash off the stress, then have a couple of beers and my sandwich. I turn in early with the alarm set for 5:15 a.m. I don't plan on eating and that should be plenty of time.

Like most nights before a new assignment, sleep is fitful and I awaken several times to check the clock. Finally the alarm goes off. I get up, shower, and hit the road.

Backing out is no problem, I shove off with my leg out the door and the car sidles backwards. I push on the gearshift and, as first gear lightly engages, get under way.

Back at the site, I stop near the gate shack, tell the new crew who I am, and drop off my bag and gear. I then park the car a little distance away from the others in the lot so a tow truck has easy access.

It's right around 6:00 a.m. when I walk up the gangplank to my new rig. I can see why the guys said they knew nuttin' 'bout no boat Bayou. The rig is docked. The gangplank wends around taped off portions of the rig where work in progress creates safety hazards. My bag is heavy and I end up throwing it over my shoulder to get through the maze.

On board I sign in, give the tool pusher my passport and green card, then go to the galley. An older black guy in Taylors cook's outfit shouts, "Hallelujah! I'm gone!" and leaves. The steward, Robert, introduces himself and says I'll bunk in his room. He says I should turn in; my first shift will be that night at six o'clock. I ask him when he wants me on deck and he says six o'clock is fine. Usually I come in early to help out with anything that needs doing and get caught up for the shift ahead.

I draw some sheets and a blanket and make my rack. It's a four-man room with a shower and a commode, but only two of the bunks are taken. The room is in the section of the rig that would be considered "officer's row," on the main floor, just down the stairs from the operations center.

Ordinarily the catering crew wouldn't occupy such refined quarters, but because the rig's in dock, there's only a handful of drill crew while the shipyard workers do the refit work.

I inherit a lower bunk, the first one in my year offshore.

Considering I've been awake for a couple of hours, I sleep surprisingly well. And long. I'm sure it has to do with yesterday's stress of losing the clutch and navigating the last 100 miles by the seat of my pants, plus last night's fitful sleep in the motel. I wake up after 3:00 p.m. and luxuriate until it's time to go on deck.

The first shift in the galley reveals there had been some excitement earlier. Workers checking the pressure on various lines had somehow connected to the galley floor drains, and when they turned the handle, the air exploded upstream and forced the pipe's contents to spew out.

"It was a shit geyser," Robert the steward deadpanned.

While not literally true, everything else in the drain of unnamable and unmentionable antecedent came bursting out. The eruption blew off the brass drain cover, which bounced off the ceiling and went rolling away clanging. A fountain of gray-brown muck erupted, four-foot high, startling Robert and the galley hand James. Both of them stared at it transfixed, horrified, and disgusted.

The geyser didn't last long—galley floor drains aren't used routinely to rid the space of excess water, only for emergency leaks and floods—so the pipes probably had just a few gallons contents. Whatever there was was now spread over two bulkheads and the food prep area. Clean-up consisted of bleach, disinfectant, mops, and detergent, and elbow grease.

I inherited clean-up of one bulkhead and an area under one prep table where plastic wrap, foil, and other dry goods were stored. It was so disgusting that I went to work right away, just to get rid of it. I removed all the things stored there, swabbed them down, and then hit the walls and floor with bleach and disinfectant. After a couple of hours, I was satisfied with the job. Even so, I used another part of the galley to make my cakes that night.

Sleeping on a rig dockside is way different than sleeping on a rig on station. On station there's always noise— throbbing and thrumming of the drilling, diesels starting and stopping, the thump turning to loud whack of choppers coming and going, plus the pounding of the roustabouts doing some God-awful, thankless task.

But dockside during the day in Texas, you have all of the above, all of the time, with the exception of the choppers. But you also have chatter and shouts in both English and Spanish, the squawk box making announcements or telling the driller to report to Control, the zip and crackle of welding on the other side of the bulkhead, the whine of sanders and the more powerful scream of their big brothers, grinders, and constant tapping, hammering and pounding, punctuated frequently by deep-in-the-bowels smashes that could only be a thirty-ton motor loosed from its rigging and crashing through the floor of the platform, killing everyone nearby and taking us all immediately to Davy Jones's (dockside) Locker, Ingleside, Texas.

Offshore, the racket is not intrusive. After a twelve-hour shift of dehumanizing toil, you'd be surprised how easy it is to fall asleep with twin eight-cylinder diesels two rooms away running at three thousand rpm making electricity.

Dockside, it's different. The racket during the day is varied, uncadenced, non-anticipatable, and persistent. It is not a soporific.

Once on a Monday early afternoon, the noise was so astounding as to be a work of art. It brought me awake laughing and shaking my head at the likes of which I never heard before or since. A Cacophony, capital "C," rather than a symphony.

The crane was running, laying down a deep bass that fluctuated in tone as the operator accelerated and decelerated to effect rotation and lifting. Several generators were on, making electricity and powering the welders. Their exhausts combined to lay down a steady tenor chord. Sanders and grinders were operating inside and outside all over the rig, providing innumerable variety of hisses and buzzes, shrieks and scratches of fanciful alto and soprano riffs. And plumbers, pipe-fitters, carpenters, mechanics, and laborers were hammering and tapping, chiseling and sledging on various metals aboard to provide irregular, but unmistakable, percussion accentual notes and pings.

One dictionary defines cacophony as "harsh discordance of sound; dissonance: *a cacophony of hoots, cackles, and wails.*" Another, further on: "Music. Frequent use of discords of a harshness and relationship difficult to understand."

Todco 205 Refit Cacophony wouldn't play so well in a symphony hall as it was loud and dissonant, discordant and harsh, non-linear and impenetrable. But it wasn't difficult to understand. It was the sound of men working to refit a mighty engine that they would float more than a thousand miles away to pierce the earth's crust ten thousand feet below and recover some of her bounty. It was the sound of industry.

I marveled at the "music," then reset my earplugs, adjusted my sleep mask, and snuggled down amidst the blankies for a couple hours more kip. I slept well, a happy little cog in an industrial undertaking.

Todco 205 in dock turned out to be a pretty desirable gig. The crew was small, with twenty to thirty eating. Transients for the company, like drivers, deliverymen, contractors, and consultants, added to the numbers. Occasionally, one of the shipyard workers would pass through the galley en route to his task and hawk a piece of chicken or a handful of cookies.

We had decent supplies, mostly because the grocery orders were for a full seventy-man crew, but also because dockside, obtaining supplies was so easy: Go get them. Robert did just that when he went to Wal-Mart for new knives and some kitchen gadgets and utensils.

The meals were solidly good, too. The steward was a graduate of the famed Culinary Institute of America, Poughkeepsie, New York. In addition to working as a chef in restaurants around the country, he had worked as executive chef at Jimmy's Harborside in Boston, which just happened to be one of my father's favorite restaurants. I hadn't been in decades, but Jimmy's was a marker of Keefe family success, if not joy. My family went there on special occasions—once or twice celebrating a notable legal victory for the patriarch and for my sister's graduation from nursing school.

Robert's meals were carefully prepared, looked gorgeous, and tasted even better. He was the only offshore cook I knew who didn't incinerate steaks on Steak Day. He'd pull the meat the day before so it had plenty of time to thaw, then he'd cook it on the hot top grill. (We couldn't use the charcoal grill because dockside, the paint and construction presented too much of a safety hazard.) Like cooking steaks at home, three or four minutes a side. When a guy asked for a medium steak, he actually *got* a medium steak—pink, hot center—not a well-done steak that was only slightly less well-done than its overcooked and desiccated neighbor.

I was more than a little surprised, both at his confidence and the icon-shattering notion of properly cooking a steak. Part of it was his skill and experience, but part of it was his brash Massachusetts manner. If a guy asked for a "medium" steak and got one cooked as it's supposed to be then bitched about it being undercooked, Robert would fix him with a glance and not-so-patiently explain that a medium steak was pink-hot center. "That is a medium steak," he'd say. "If ya wanted something else, you didn't want it medium."

I overcooked steaks routinely. I knew I was sinning against St. Lawrence and the laws of steakhouses from coast to coast, and especially Texas, but offshore cookery in some things is more hash house than steakhouse. Plus, my early Steak Day experiences having the pink-center steaks thrown out, demonstrated to me that well-done is what the guys want. When Maria, the laundress on Marianas, told me her Keefe-cooked steak was dry and tough, I offered her another, which she refused. Inside I thought, "Yeah, I know. Awful, isn't it? But it's how it's done."

Through personnel turmoil, I inherited Robert's galley hand, James, who was mid forties and had a career in demolition—crowbar and sledge, not explosives—in California before returning to his home state of Louisiana and going offshore. He aspired to be a steward, so he was happy to lend a hand cooking. He needed more experience and practice and thoughtful supervision—time seemed to get away from him.

One night he decided to make turnovers. We were caught up in work and I was finishing my baking, so the ovens were clear. The project was a labor of love, hand-kneading the dough vigorously, with surprising and unexpectedly huge douses of oil and making a lard-based confectioner's cream to complement the preserves center. It took nearly three hours exclusive of cooking time. The final product was unusual, odd-shaped, and irregular, yet tasty. They ranged in size from small dinner plates to full-blown Frisbees, and the crewman who ate one would have an eight thousand-calorie jump-start on a ten thousand-calorie day. Robert saw them the next morning and nodded in unspoken assessment, but then added that it was important for James to pay attention to size since consuming one would probably result in the diner not having to eat for the rest of the week.

Because the crew was small, there was time to experiment with desserts. James had some recipes he had printed, and I used them for a couple different kinds of cookies. His recipe for sugar drop cookies did pretty well a couple times around. I added a dollop of strawberry preserves in the center and they resembled shortbread cookies with jam. A coffee-flavored cake from the back of the Domino confectioners sugar box did very well a trio of times around, and a Steen's cane syrup cake from the label of the can probably made one old boy weep and think of home and grandma. The cake was a cross between hell, Boston brown bread, and Saturday night in a sharecropper's cabin in winter, 1880. Thick, dense, moist, heavy, and reminiscent of molasses, with no frosting and very little else to redeem it except stomach-loading and bowel-clogging heft, the cake could only appeal to someone carrying a certain heritable gene or memories of a childhood growing up impoverished, but loved, in Mississippi. The cake damn sure broadened the dessert repertoire, but we only "sold" two or three slices of it.

After a week or so, reconstruction was sufficiently far enough along to try out the systems. It's a good idea to make sure things work the way they're supposed to in dry dock with the means at hand to fix what doesn't work, rather than try to jack-up at sea and discover in the midst of twelve-foot waves that the hydraulic gazinter can't properly engage with the lift and separate mechanism. The jack-up process began with accompanying whines and howls from machinery, and Todco 205 began to climb.

Rated for water depth of two hundred feet, the rig has three legs that rival the derrick for visual predominance. Standing on the deck and looking up, the legs tower over you. You don't realize how tall they are until you get to the top and look out. The climbing process seemed to last about a day. It started when I was off shift. On shift, I'd periodically stick my nose out to see what was what and where we were. I could gauge progress by the sight of the huge production platform under construction next door. From sea level at the dock, the platform reigned over us. Men took a crane-powered elevator to get to its decks to work. Emerging to cross the gangplank, they looked to be a half-inch tall. When the 205 reached the limit of its climb, we were looking down twenty-five, thirty feet or more to the platform. The view of Ingleside and environs was impressive, not so much for the scenery—Ingleside was dusty, gritty industrial Texas—but for the panorama provided by two hundred plus feet of altitude.

The climb down marked the beginning of the end of our time in dock. Descending seemed to take about a day, too. With a successful jack-up and jack-down, final preparations for the tow began. Workmen detached hoses and lines, cleaned up, painted, and carried tools and gear off the rig. The crane was busy lifting off machines and welders and bringing aboard pallets of supplies and other stuff. In the galley, we took on additional groceries, including a huge load of canned soda and numerous cases of Wolf brand chili, both of which were toted up to the second floor, flag-officers' quarters, and stacked in the hallway. The soda was for the American crew once on station. The chili, an oilfield staple since Texas first created oilfields, was apparently one of the boss's must-have foods.

A day or so later, tugboats were maneuvering around the rig when I went off shift; and, when I came back on twelve hours later and looked out, we were south of Corpus, a mile or two offshore, and the shipyard was long gone in our wake.

The car had to be dealt with, but there was no urgency because we weren't going anywhere for a while. Early on, I decided to forget it for a few days while I acquainted

myself with the routine on the rig. After a week, I was broken in and ready to have a go. With a little help from No. 2
son back in Connecticut, I obtained the name of a Saab dealer in the Houston area. The experience was instructive, if for
nothing other than trying to write on a notepad balanced on
my knee, tiny cell phone precariously jammed between ear
and shoulder while scrunched over on the lower bunk.

As a former newspaper reporter and editor, I was
well versed in taking notes while talking on the phone. In the
newsroom or the office, my phones were usually equipped
with some stick-on or strap-on device that allowed me to
comfortably lodge the handset between my shoulder and my
ear. A slight cock of the head was all the physical contortion
it took to lock the handset in place and to leave the hands
free for keyboarding.

Hard to do with a cell phone. Engineers, anticipating users' needs and realizing the device was too tiny to use
it like an AT&T bakelite handset, came up with a variety
of accessories to enable hands-free use—ear jacks and buds,
cute little microphones and mouth sets—but I owned none
of it, just the cell phone.

Resorting to type, it is possible to cradle a cell phone
between your head and shoulder, and a mere inclination of
the head is enough to lock it in place. Given the size of the
phone, however, it's really more like it's wedged into your
neck rolls, the receiver is positioned under your earlobe, and
the speaker is adjacent to your larynx, or jowl, for the over
fifty set. This wouldn't matter too much if earlobes could
hear and jowls could speak, but alas, such is not the case.

After a lot of back and forth between Texas and
Connecticut, then Ingleside and Houston, and after a fair

amount of dropped calls, as well as dropped phones, arrangements were set for a tow truck to come down, pick up my damaged goods, then return it to the dealer for repairs. That, too, was complicated by a tow truck breakdown and then a day of bad weather, but finally the show was on. The driver, after motoring around lost in Ingleside, found the site much as I had and pulled up next to the parked car. Celebrating our rendezvous like the U.S. Army meeting the Russians on the Elbe in '45, we clasped hands and slapped backs like good ole comrades. Mission Sorta Acomplished. He loaded up Blackie Jr., said "So long!" and departed for home, while I shuffled back to the rig and bed, imagining a trail of my dollar bills marking passage of the truck and cargo from here to there.

I guess it must be Texas, but everything about the trip to Mexico seems larger than life. The 205 itself is of considerable bulk, but it hardly seems imposing enough to require three mighty ocean-going tugboats to locomote it. Nevertheless, there they were, working steadily if not full power, to make headway. The speed—three knots—is absolutely serene. Ocean swells move faster and you can watch them overtake us, but with the heft of the rig, there is very little motion as they pass underneath. Occasionally one will hit perfectly with a considerable impact and judder; and the deck is always wet and frequently awash. Smokers need to be alert because a good dousing is only a second's nonvigilance away. But the speed is implacable, too. You're not going fast, but you are going far, more than eighty-miles per day. On a 1,100-mile trip, it will take two weeks steaming, but each passing hour presents a different vista.

We remain close to the shore—it's always in sight until well into Mexico approaching the oilfields. The tugs lead the way like a Roman triga, the chariot drawn with three horses abreast. I'm impressed with their coordination and the skill with which the captains maintain their position. In a heaving sea—the most fluid of environments—the difficulty of holding course is manifest. This trio is rock solid. They may be screaming and cursing at each other on the radio, but I don't think so. I think computers, autopilots, and GPS have reduced the human element to wary boredom.

Considerable tow cable is involved, too. There looks to be a minimum of one hundred yards between us and them. The force and resistance can be estimated when the wind is right and the cables hum a tenor note with tension. Sometimes the sea washes over the cables, but that is a function of swells; the cables are never slack.

Two and a half days into the tow we stop and jack up. The weather report is trending badly: storms, high seas, and wind. Worse farther south. It takes a few hours, but eventually we're secure high above the water. The tugs anchor off us in staggered rows, their bows to windward.

After three days of sitting, there's grumbling and murmuring. The weather passed without much unpleasantness, and last night a rival rig under tow heading south motored past. That didn't sit too well with the Todco guys. I heard, "How come we're sitting here and the Diamond rig is under way!?" more than once.

Then, after announcing we were about to climb down again, the decision was made to put it off for twenty-four hours because of high seas. The mat sitting on the ocean floor is attached to legs, and they couldn't be retracted fast enough to prevent possible wave action from slamming it against the bottom and possibly wrecking it. Strategically, it was unquestionably the right decision. Tactically, it was unquestionably wrong.

During the jack-up, departure day for the Todco skeleton crew came and went. They had been on board for twenty-eight days, and with each passing day, their time ashore and at home diminished, or so they said, and the sooner they'd be returning. Although they were being paid, after four weeks of twelve-hour days (even when the routine isn't as rigorous as drilling on station) they were fatigued; they were homesick; and they'd had enough.

From my notebook:

Halloween 2:00 a.m.-ish
Seventeenth day. We're still up in the air. At shift change, the sun was out and the wind was down and the temps up. Rollers rolling, but they sure didn't look threatening to me. But what do I know? Rumor and smart word is back to tow Thursday—just under twenty-four hours. We've been here since Friday midnight into Saturday.

Scuttlebutt is it's Hercules HQ in Houston; it's a chance to get some more stuff squared away; it's fear of the weather. Tho' the wind has been steady for several days—twenty plus, I'd guesstimate—the ocean wasn't so awfully rough. But here we sit.

I'm lethargic and not too almighty caring. I sleep a lot. And I am on shift a lot, but I'm not constantly working. I do a few baked things and keep up, but I'm not maniacal about cleaning or anything else.

Halloween 7:40 p.m.-ish
Turned in this morning with prep ongoing for descent and tow. Got up after the whole day's sleep—7:00 – 11:30; 11:30 – 3:40 and 4:00 – 5:40—to find we're still descending but preparing to get under way.

That stopped at 7:00 a.m. when the occasional roller sparked fear of smashing the mat against the sea floor and making a racket/danger. The day was beautiful and calm, and there were rollers (four to six feet), but not white caps, just swells. Fear was, couldn't get legs up quick enough to prevent a serious bounce that could cause serious . . . what? Anyhow, they called it off and everyone became gloomier.

It's a funny state. The crew was supposed to change yesterday, and they face ten or so more days. We're pariahs and jokers, so we don't count and don't figure in the mix. But the uncertainty is wearing people down.

I'm ambivalent but lethargic. I'm thinking off by Veterans Day and come what will. So there's sort of a self-styled terminus. I don't feel pressure to get off. I'd like to be off work, but I'm pretty good about anxiety and other manias.

My fingernail has grown out since I shaved it at SONOCO six weeks ago this Friday. It should be all grown out by week-end/Monday. I stopped using Neosporin on burns/bashes—especially the thumb hang-nail/bash—and things seem to be responding nicely. But it could be they're responding to natural healing after a week or so past.

Need more thought on the lethargy. . . .

Need to think on what to make for dessert. . . .

Friday Nov. 2 7:31 p.m.
So the official word is we'll be there Wednesday. Scuttlebutt is we're going five knots. I think it's wearing pretty heavily on everyone.

I'm dickin' the dawg tonight. There's a half tray of cookies and half a cake out, plus the main tray of cookies, for dessert. I could do a throw-away cobbler for breakfast plus some Rice Krispie treats and be done with it.

I'm still interested in exploring the nature of lethargy, but I'm too phlegmatic.

Sunday Nov. 4 7:33 p.m.
Nice breakfast this morning. Saturday night I worked a lot: rolls, Rice Krispie treats, chocolate cake, sugar jam cookies, cinnamon buns, and scrambled cheese burrito.

Had deep down hunger—been eating a lot of sugar and Fudgesicles, and walloped a burrito with a sausage patty in it. Good.

Robert had bad tidings at nine-ish when I got up after rolling around.

So the tidings were get there Tuesday/ Wednesday, then dick the dawg for four to five days inspection, plus catering crew horseshit, then out probably Monday or Tuesday at eleven or twelve o'clock. Veterans Day!

It was a little discouraging because for a couple of days it seemed like it could be Wednesday or Thursday this week.

After annoyance, I'm over it. The trip ends when it ends. . . .

But circumstances worsened as frustrations mounted, communication failed, and idiocy reigned.

Chili

No oilfield adventure would be complete without a word about chili. Like the corndog, its importance can't be overstated. In the above chapter, just what chili means was demonstrated in the case after case of Wolf chili we loaded before leaving Ingleside for Campeche. And that was the allotment for one of the bosses!

Cans of chili could be found in the storeroom of almost every rig. But cans didn't play such a big role in food service offshore because chili is easy to make and homemade is better. Once again, the styles were varied, although the most common was hamburger, onion and garlic, chili powder and spices, and tomato sauce for a simple red chili to dress up hot dogs and provide the meat for tacos.

The recipe below is a real Texas red: meat, no beans, and no tomato. You can limit the knife work by cutting larger squares. But it might not meet International Chili Society cook-off standards!

The other recipe is for an emergency when chili is necessary and you've only got a half hour.

Texas Red
3 pounds of decent beef, trimmed and cut into ⅓-inch cubes
1 cup flour
1 teaspoon kosher salt
1 teaspoon ground black pepper
¼ cup oil (I like canola.)
1 onion diced
4 cloves garlic smashed
4 tablespoons chili powder (I like Gebhardt brand.)
2 tablespoons ground cumin
1 tablespoon oregano
1 tablespoon dried parsley
1 teaspoon paprika
2 bay leaves
½ tablespoon cayenne
Tony Chachere's
1 cup strong black coffee
1 quart beef broth (Commercial is OK.)

Put a good stew pot on medium heat and add oil. Pour flour, salt, and pepper in a bag, add half the beef cubes, and shake to coat. When oil is ready, brown the meat. When one batch is seared, do the remaining meat. Save the flour in the bag. You can use it as a slurry later to thicken your chili if necessary.

You can add a little oil to the pot if the first batch soaked it all up. Or you can add a little water. Stir. When the second batch is browned, take it out and add it to the first. Toss the onion and garlic into the pot, stir, and let it wilt a little. Return the meat to the pot, then add the chili powder, cumin, oregano, dried parsley, paprika, Tony Chachere's, and cayenne.

Add the coffee and stir, and then add just enough beef broth to cover. Turn heat down and let simmer for two hours. Add beef broth as needed, stirring occasionally. Taste. Adjust spices and salt and pepper to taste before serving.

This is a great meal for breakfast, lunch, or dinner. Garnishes, like raw onion, sliced jalapeno, or grated cheese, only make it better. Accompaniments range from eggs, tortillas, and coffee for breakfast, to Texas toast or cornbread, a tossed salad and beer for other meals.

Enjoy!

Emergency chili
1 pound hamburger (I like ground sirloin at 85 percent lean to 15 percent fat.)
3 tablespoons olive oil
½ onion diced
2 cloves garlic smashed
½ cup water
3 tablespoons chili powder
1 tablespoons ground cumin
1 bay leaf
Tony Chachere's
½ teaspoon cayenne
½ teaspoon oregano
½ teaspoon dried parsley
1 can red kidney beans
1 jar hot salsa

Salt and pepper to taste

Brown hamburger in oil. Pour off liquid and set meat aside. In a hot pan, wilt onion and garlic. When translucent, add back meat. Add water and spices and stir. When bubbling, add beans. Rinse bean can with a little water and add that to chili. Add salsa. Let cook on medium-low for 10 to 15 minutes. Salt and pepper to taste.

CHAPTER 10

Denouement

"Don't get stuck on stupid!" General Russel Honore said to reporters in the wake of Hurricane Katrina.

I've found, indeed discovered in myself, that if you're in a stressful situation for a while, your sense and sensibility begins to erode. By stressful, I don't mean balancing work and family, getting to work on time despite a hellish commute, or gaining three pounds so that your "hips" are noticeably larger, when in fact you mean your ass.

No. This stress is existing in less-than-ideal circumstances when you'd rather be doing something—Anything! —else, and there's no compelling reason not to, except you're hostage to the situation. Which, in this case, specifically refers to the endless tow of Todco 205 to Mexico.

By the first weekend of November, many, Todco crew *and* Taylors crew, were getting stuck on stupid.

As your stupidity increases, your good will declines. You lose your level-headedness and become unbalanced. Base emotions take hold; little things grate on you; and you're no longer willing to indulge someone's quirks.

Only through molar-crushing effort can you restrain your-self from having at them recklessly in word, or possibly felo-niously, in deed.

Rumors, which you'd ordinarily ignore, sneak through your intellectual armor and infect you, provoking more stupid and unholy reaction. Speculation and ignorant talk from the unknowing you'd ordinarily dismiss as morons and cretins takes seed and sprouts poisonous shoots.

You hear the Mexican customs officials are coming aboard and they'll be searching rooms and confiscating lap-tops, CD players, and cell phones. You look forward to the former—it means something is happening to end the tow; and you get angry at the latter—the high-handed son-of-a-bitches, when in fact you mean sons-of-bitches, the stupidity of which angers you even more.

Confiscation does in fact occur, which is why the briefings tell you not to bring laptops, CD players, and cell phones into Mexico. But you forget or ignore it and bring them anyways, because, after all, you're an American. Well, you've just made Sergeant Garcia's and Lieutenant Rodri-go's day, boosting them with your generosity into the ranks of the wealthy Mexicans who possess laptops and Sony CD players.

The Mexicans who do come aboard, are from Petroleos Mexicanos (Pemex) the state-owned oil company that chartered the rig. They're not doing anything substan-tive that anyone can see, just yakking and gassing and jaw-boning.

Some Mexican crew members are coming aboard, too, a handful at a time, so that after a number of days, surprisingly, the dining room at midnight is full of orange-jumpsuit-clad Pemex workers.

Our destination isn't referred to on the rig by name. When anyone talks about it, it's called the "Pemex oilfields off Campeche." That's more a description, however, than a place name.

The place we're going is the Cantarell Complex in the Bay of Campeche, Gulf of Mexico, off the coast of Yucatan. The oil field is about fifty miles northwest of Ciudad del Carmen, a city of 150,000 in the state of Campeche. The cool thing about the oil field is its geology. The formation from which the oil is extracted was created when the Chicxulub meteor plowed into the earth. Right. The dinosaur-eliminating meteor.

Approaching the oilfield at night is best because it is a sight to behold. In fact, it is a sight visible from space or one of the NASA night shots of earth. The field shows as a dot of light off Yucatan, surrounded by oceans of darkness.

Back on earth, approaching the field from miles away, there is an orange tint to the horizon. It's similar to the glow of an urban area. Recognizable as some kind of light illuminating the night sky, it's also weird and unsettling because the color is unusual, a more sinister, deeper orange than the common yellow-orange glow of vapor lights. With each passing hour, the tint grows brighter and higher in the sky until at some point you come sufficiently over the curve of the earth to behold orange dots of light filling 150 or 160 degrees of horizon ahead of you. What th' hell? Then you realize: It's fire! And indeed it is. With another hour's towing, the dots become individual flares, seventeen or twenty of them creating the spectacle. Closer still, and you have an idea of the monstrous size of these flares flickering and dancing. The air is perfumed with the thick scent of hydro-carbons.

MMMMmmmm!

Depending upon how severely depressed your morale is, or how obstinately stuck on stupid you are from having been at work for weeks on end with no respite and none in sight either (in this third-world foreign country that's going to take away your computer and tunes) you might be thinking in your current self-pitying-state that it's appropriate your destination should be hell, full of fire, and bear the scent of burning flesh.

Yup. Perdition, Mexico.

Feeling clever, but temporarily insane, you might even relate the hellish scene to the meteor that killed off an entire reptilian race and helped create the oil field, and intuit some faintly logical, hysterical, yet emotionally appealing and self-congratulatory, green analogy about the end of the dinosaurs and the flares heralding the end of us because of some damn thing that's bad. Y'know carbon, or hydrocarbon, or gasoline or the automobile, global warming, or human endeavor . . . something!

Nonsense!

The reason you think the scene is hell is because all your life you've been told anything having to do with scary fire or appalling and uncontrolled flame *is* hell. Forest fires in California. Mount St. Helens. Mount Pinatubo. Chernobyl. The burning oil fields of Kuwait Saddam touched off in 1991.

Well, if Kuwait in '91 was hell, the answer to that nightmare is hire Red Adair, Boots & Coots, and Wild Well Control, Inc., to put the fires out. Like the Kuwaitis did, offer generous amounts of cash and oodles more as incentive pay, and in a matter of weeks those boys will own markers for most of your fortune and have Hades itself extinguished. Then we can get on with extracting and using the once-blazing resources of hell to break oil cartels, bolster crude supply, lower prices, and improve humanity, not punish us.

The Cantarell Field is cool.

So we jack up for a while, then we jack down and tow over to another spot where we jack up and still nothing happens. Day follows night, and more Mexican workers come aboard. Coming on shift, or just having arrived by crew boat, they hit the midnight meal, and that Gringo grub appeals to them. They compliment me on the cooking and are vocal indeed about my homemade Buffalo wings. Every freakin' one is gone, and some of those boys, wolfish and lean, look like they're going to lick the pan. One brave soul, getting in the spirit of things American and cookhouse warm and fuzzy, asks for a three-egg omelet. I'm sufficiently stern and grumpy to slam the door, so-to-speak, on that particular camel's nose under the tent by replying the grill's not on and I can't get it going soon enough. "Omelette demain," I say in the first foreign language that comes to mind, "pour la petit dejeuner," mangling the article but nodding and smiling. "Hmmmmm," my diners seem to reflect. "French, hunh?" Maybe they think I'm a descendant of Maximilian's troops their great-great-grandfathers whipped at Puebla on Cinco de Mayo, '62. "Bueno!" they agree, nodding, smiling, and waving. Then they get it: "That dumb-ass must be a Cajun," they think, heading off to work.

The tugs leave. One shift they're there; the next, they're gone. So apparently we are where we need to be. Still not too much appears to be happening, or no one seems to know too much about it. Wednesday, a big boss from Pemex moves on board. His arrival points towards some progress.

Two-oh-five is a Todco rig, even despite that company being bought by Hercules earlier in the year. The Todco culture is alive and well, and that's clear when the local bosses stop by. Hercules bosses wear blue overalls with Hercules badges on the shoulder or left chest, and occasionally, Hercules in letters across the back. Todco bosses' overalls are red. When the Todco crew bringing the rig down meet up with the locals—both Pemex *and* Hercules—they put on new red overalls, an unmistakable statement of who they are, what their history is, and, be there no doubt, where their loyalties lie. Their paychecks might read "Hercules," but this is a Todco crew.

The tool pusher, the guy responsible for rig operations, is a considerable chunk of man. Most of the time he's in pink overalls, elderly Todco issue that's faded through a hundred washes, but there's nothing "pink" about this guy at all. Forty-eight to fifty-three years old I'd guess. Maybe six feet, three inches, 260 pounds or so. Thick torso *not* gone to fat, forearms thrusting out of the sleeves of the coveralls like ships cables, and round head with cropped brown hair and brown weather-beaten face. The pusher isn't reluctant in the middle of addressing a roomful of crew and caterers to stop, lean over a wastebasket, and let go a spew of tobacco juice that would have impressed Josey Wales. That he was willing to do so in such a manner and setting says more about *your* delicacies than his, I reckon.

Midweek, the pusher calls his men into the lounge. They close the door and he briefs them on what's going to happen, or at least theoretically what's supposed to happen. This is Mexico, after all!

No one bothers to tell the caterers. No update, no briefing, no info, no nothing. Not that anyone's obliged to, mind you. The caterers are contractors and are there until they're relieved. That's one way of seeing it. But if you start with a pack of simpletons, after a month or so when even your ordinary folk and dependable crew members are muttering and fixing to eat their own, a visual assessment of the simpletons who make your food and bed would reveal they are nearly tipped over into lunacy. That's not good for your command.

Things from the briefing leak out, and the rumors spread among the caterers. One position seems firm and non-negotiable. A Mexican catering crew is being together. They will arrive when they do. Until then, the catering crew aboard the rig will make meals, make beds, and do laundry, as well as prepare the rig for hand-over. Hold your questions, nobody tells us, because there aren't any answers.

That is a perfectly sensible position. It is not sensitive, but sensitivity is generally in short supply on oil drilling rigs. It's also sufficiently hard and ham-fisted to loose the incipient insanity that's been infecting the catering crew for a week now.

James, an impressionable sort, is taking pictures of supposed abuses on his cell phone and laying the groundwork for his federal lawsuit for which he will receive damages for kidnapping, unlawful restraint, piracy, perjury, hate crimes, unethical behavior, psychic pain, and possibly full moon menstrual cramps. Robert, in the middle of lunch and without a word to anyone, finds a novelized copy of a Tom Clancy spin-off video game, leaves the galley and goes into the storeroom, opens the door, sits down, lights a butt, and starts reading. I come into the galley at noon, unable to sleep, panting pathologically over non-exertion, and start eating Blue Belle ice cream bars because all the Fudgesicles are gone, staring with loathing at the character on the box who's supposed to be dressed like a farmer, but really looks like a barnyard queen from Hayside.

That's the high-end response. Below decks, the bedroom hands are slobbering imbeciles blatantly and unashamedly taking naps in the middle of shift on hard benches in the crew's changing/smoking room. They scatter like roaches when the red coveralls come in, catch them, and start bawling; yet there's an element of fearlessness, too. They remind me of the storied GI outside the orderly room of one besieged fire base in the Central Highlands in 1969. Standing there in his skivvies, drunk, and smoking a joint, the dude's buddies told him to skedaddle. If the captain or the first sergeant saw him, he'd end up in trouble. "Whatta they gonna do," he mumbled, "send me to 'Nam?"

The stupidity peaked Friday during the noon meal. Robert was on. Fritz, the dayside bedroom hand who slept in our room, was in the galley, as was I, being unable to sleep.

We were having a grumble session when Luis, the Mexican Hercules big boss, walked by.

"I need to find out about this," Robert said. So he beckoned to Luis.

We hadn't met him, so Robert pointed us out and said our names. Luis acknowledged each with a slight nod.

"We want to get off the rig," Robert said. Subtlety and nuance are not Robert's strong points.

Luis looked at him, startled.

"We want to get off the rig right now," Robert repeated, a little louder and somewhat agitated.

Luis nodded his head once, sharply. Angry now. "Put it in writing," he said, turned, and walked out.

That was it. The wave of stupidity that had been building for nearly two weeks now had crested and broke.

Robert, Fritz, and I began to dither.

The truth of it is, we did want to get off. Robert had been aboard for eight and possibly ten weeks by then. James, seven or eight. I was on my twenty-seventh day, and Fritz had been aboard for longer than a month. I didn't really have any "demands" other than to find out what was planned for us. I did want to get off, and a day or two would be fine, three would be acceptable, but not much more than that. Most of all, I wanted some information: a firm timetable for the end of it.

Robert's declaration instantly shifted the situation into a confrontation.

My stupidity peaked next.

"What are we going to write?" Fritz asked.

I tore a page from the galley notebook and wrote "We, the undersigned, want to get off the rig immediately."

I showed it to them. They nodded.

I signed it, leaving a couple of lines above my signature so Robert could sign it first as steward. Robert took it, looked at it, and signed his name below mine. Fritz signed his below Robert's.

James wouldn't sign it, nor would any of the other hands.

"Hmmmmm," I thought. First off, so much for Mr. Keefe, the corporate spokesman, trained in crisis communication, adept at wordsmithing and parsing phraseology so the egregious is merely distasteful. When it counted, the capability failed; and my ill-considered statement compounded Robert's willfulness and lack of tact.

The other interesting aspect was the instant cessation of complaint, bitch, whine, and avowal of solidarity from the bedroom hands. When it came time to put your name to something, all the posturing, talk of federal lawsuits, and tellin' Th' Man what for evaporated as soon as the hammer of the gun cocked. When it came time to put up or shut up, they shut up!

Robert sought out and gave the paper to Luis. I returned to the room and my bed and slept well thinking, "Well, we'll be getting off this slab pretty quickly. . . ."

Coming on shift at 5:45 p.m., I exited the room as the tool pusher was coming down the stairs from the operations center. James was with him and a clutch of Taylors red-shirts.

"Cook!" he called out. I stopped.

"Yes sir!" I answered. He came up, the Taylors boys behind him in a gaggle.

"You want off?" he said, looking at me. It wasn't threatening, but it wasn't friendly either. I believe it was the first words he spoke to me on the trip. I thought a second.

"Yes sir," I replied. "I signed on to bring the rig to

Mexico, and we're in Mexico. I've been on a month tomorrow, but I was told it would be a twenty-one-day tow. I've had enough. It's time to go in."

We looked at each other. Conversation over, I turned and left.

The evening meal was sort of weird. Robert and Fritz made themselves scarce just after relief, so it was James and me in the galley. Some of the day bosses, including the tool pusher, remained at the Todco table yakking with the night crew and bosses. Their eyes were on me when I came out to clean the milk machine or make fresh coffee, straighten out the line, or pass through the dining room to the storeroom to fetch something.

When the day bosses and the night pusher left, and the dining room was empty, Hippie, the driller, and Cajun, the crane operator, started singing "Fifteen men on a dead man's chest." These were the guys for whom I'd made the midnight meal for four weeks and I knew them fairly well. I liked them. I think they liked me. They ate my grub and didn't complain; in fact, they usually had seconds.

I laughed, got a cup of coffee, and went over to the table to tell them my side of it. It was easy. I said I signed on to bring the rig to Mexico and we were in Mexico. Now it's time to get off. They agreed. I said I figured it'd take a couple of days to get things squared away, and that I wasn't planning on going anywhere soon. They just looked at me.

I jokingly explained the difference between piracy and mutiny, incorrectly pointing out that mutiny could only occur in time of war. I likened my situation more to a "forced resignation" than mutiny. Hippie asked if I had been a teacher. I said no, but I read a lot.

It was mutiny.

James was sorrowful. Usually voluble, verbal, and manic, that night he was silent, doing his chores. A couple of times he said, "I wish you wouldn't go." Finally I replied, "James, this is a good opportunity. You want to be a steward, and now you will. With Robert and me gone, you can run the place. You'll show Hector (the Taylors supervisor who often was the subject of his prattling on and who worked with and frequently vexed him) what you can do, and this will help you achieve what you want."

I was only half-lying.

Midnight meal came and went. The evening tool pusher was a little frosty, but he was second in command and probably got an earful from the day pusher. Hippie and Cajun were wary, not entirely cordial, but surely not hateful either. They left, and the Mexicans came in and cleaned the line out. James broke it down at 1:00 a.m., and I went in and started to frost my cake.

About 1:20 a.m., the night pusher came in and said, "Your boat's here. Go tell the other guys, collect your shit, and take off."

The night pusher was a Christian gentleman, and I hadn't heard him cuss in a month of meals. I was surprised.

"Whatta ya mean the boat's here?" I said. "I'm in the middle of my shift." I was truly taken unaware that things had happened as fast as they did. Surprisingly, even in Mexico, the demand to be taken of a rig "immediately" apparently means "right freakin' now."

"Well, you said wanted to get off," the night pusher said not kindly, "so now you can get off. . . ."

I was about to protest, but then I got . . . stubborn?

Enlightened? I took off my apron, grabbed my knives, note-book, and Albertson's plastic attaché bag, and went to the room. I woke up Robert and Fritz and told them a boat was here to take us off. Robert bounded out of bed to open his locker, taking a few things and throwing them in a bag. He was ready in minutes. He left most of his Taylors issue and some other togs he'd gotten at Wal-Mart in Corpus.

Fritz and I took a little more time to pack. I took everything, including hardhat and life preserver, and Fritz cleaned out his locker pretty thoroughly as well.

But we were all ready in twenty minutes. We didn't sign out, the normal procedure when departing a rig. We just left. Some more Mexican crewmen who had come out on the boat and were chattering and in pantomime told us it was a sloppy ride and that we'd all be seasick. The night pusher and Hippie were on deck and Cajun was driving the crane. I told the night pusher I hadn't expected things to be this abrupt and I was sorry for an unsatisfactory ending. He didn't say anything. We boarded the Billy Pugh basket and Cajun lifted us down to the boat.

Hippie was standing at the rail smoking a butt. I looked up and waved. He didn't respond but just looked at me.

The trip back was rough. I don't know that the skip-per had been instructed to make it rough and make it last, but it took four hours to get us to port, a trip that on an American crewboat would have taken just over two. There was a lot of back and forth and up and down, but with only three of us heading in, we could all lie down and no one got sick.

We got into Ciudad del Carmen around sunup. The

boat dropped us off at a dock, then turned around and went someplace else. We had no instruction and no good idea of what to do. We argued briefly about a course of action, then we decided to go to the airport to see if we could learn anything there. That was a bust at 6:30 a.m., and after an hour we decided to go to the Holiday Inn that served as the staging point for Todco/Hercules in the city.

At the hotel, Robert saw one of the bosses from the relief crew for 205 and asked him what to do. The guy introduced him to a Mexican gopher who would make the necessary arrangements for us to leave. We were told to get a room, clean up, and that we'd be taking off later in the day.

That's what I did and took a nap. Robert and Fritz went out for a couple of beers, but we all met at the airport, got our passports checked, and got seats on the Continental flight to Houston's Bush International.

At the airport in Texas, we parted company. Robert and Fritz were returning to Corpus Christi. Fritz was from Brownsville and would get home from there, and Robert's truck was at the Kiewit Dock. We shook hands and walked out of each other's lives.

I rented a car and drove south to the part of town with proximity to the Saab dealer where Blackie Jr. was. Since it was sundown Saturday, I had all of Sunday to spare. I found a Comfort Inn, had a nice Thai supper in a local restaurant, and tried to relax and act normally. I didn't sleep well, had weird dreams, and wasn't too happy with how things worked out.

There was an element of guilt. I've never walked off a job before or quit like that—and I didn't like it. I truly didn't expect things to happen as fast as they did, which I guess makes me naïve at best or more profoundly stuck on stupid than I thought.

I was also unsure of how things would work out on the rig—although it was partly of my doing, the solution was long-since out of my hands—and I didn't like that either.

I felt gritty and dissatisfied and mildly unhappy. But I have to confess, I was also deeply relieved to be ashore and have the trip over. Sunday I woke up at 3:00 a.m., watched infomercials, drank all the hotel room coffees, and slept for a couple hours more. Awakening, I watched some more TV, got more coffee and drank it, and moped about. Around noon, I went to the grocery store, bought peanuts, cheese, crackers, and beer, and found a decent local BBQ joint with stuff to go. A solid meal and football on the tube and beer helped perk up my spirits.

The next day early, I drove over to the Saab dealer. The car was ready. The tow was $650. The breakdown wasn't a cable, it was worse and required a new clutch to be ordered and sent from Sweden. The part cost $1,200, and the labor was around $1,800.

I brought the rental car back to the airport, caught a lift back to the dealer, paid for Blackie Jr. with plastic, checked out of the hotel, and lit a shuck for home.

Driving east, the sun was over my shoulder and I was indeed heading into a new day.

Epilogue

I grossed approximately $3,400 (including mileage one way) for the Mexico tow. Take-home was considerably less than that, around $2,400. Repairs to the car cost about $3,700 and did not include my weekend in Houston, which with auto rental, meals, two-nights lodging, and groceries, cost about $500. Nor did the outlay include the cost of lodging in Corpus before the tow.

My last communication from Taylors was a personnel action form Number 12, fired for deserting the position.

That didn't make me happy, either, because even though I quit, I knew I was fired.

So did they. . . .

Redneck Gravy

3 tablespoons butter
4 tablespoons flour
1 16-ounce can of stewed tomatoes
salt
pepper

Place a two-quart pan over medium heat and melt butter. Whisk in the flour to make a roux. Cook the roux, stirring until it reaches blonde or light brown stage. This is not the dark brown or brick red roux of a gumbo, but considerably lighter.

Open the tomatoes and dump into a bowl. Break them and the clumps up with your hands like when you make spaghetti sauce. The finer, the better. When the roux is the color you want, dump the tomatoes in and continue to stir. When the mixture boils, remove from heat and add salt and pepper to taste.

This is the R.D. Collins redneck gravy recipe, and it's decent. Serve on a fresh-baked biscuit. But it also works perfectly well on thick-sliced buttered toast.

All due respect to Mr. Collins, nevertheless, you can still doctor the mixture up. Hot sauce and hot peppers aren't offensive, and salsa adds flavor, but makes the gravy more salsa-like.

Other vegetables, like finely-diced green or sweet red peppers, onions, fresh (or canned) mushrooms, sautéed and added work well too. Those ingredients boost flavor but subvert the simple nature of this country fare.

Patrick S. Keefe is a native of Dover, New Hampshire. After a normal childhood and undistinguished, though highly-enjoyable, attendance at St. Mary Academy and St. Thomas Aquinas High School in Dover, he matriculated at the College of St. Thomas in St. Paul, Minnesota. He quit a year later, joined the army, and served as a military policeman from 1971 to 1974. Honorably discharged, he worked for a year as a federal police officer at the Veterans Administration Center in Togus, Maine, before returning to Minnesota and college in early 1976. After graduation, he moved to Connecticut in 1981 and pursued a career in journalism, starting as a newspaper correspondent at the Willimantic Chronicle and ending as assistant managing editor of the Norwich Bulletin. After a decade newspapering, he opted for regular hours and an improved salary in the Public Information Office of the University of Connecticut Health Center in Farmington, where he remained until he moved to Baton Rouge in 2006.

To earn money, he has worked as a blueberry picker, greenskeeper, construction laborer, caterer, mini-mart clerk, short-order grill man, production line worker, forklift driver, printer, day laborer, direct-mail marketer, scallop fisherman, and freelance writer.

At one point in Connecticut, he owned three chainsaws, and for a number of years he put up by hand five cords of hardwood for winter.